W9-CIA-276

CREATION
of the
MODERN MIDDLE EAST

Iraq

CREATION

of the

MODERN MIDDLE EAST

CREATION

of the

MODERN MIDDLE EAST

Iraq

Chelsea House
An imprint of Infobase Publishing
132 West 31st Street
New York NY 10001

Library of Congress Cataloging-in-Publication Data
Wagner, Heather Lehr.
  Iraq / by Heather Lehr Wagner. — 2nd ed.
    p. cm. — (Creation of the modern Middle East)
  Includes bibliographical references and index.
  ISBN 978-1-60413-021-8 (hardcover)
  1. Iraq—History—20th century—Juvenile literature. I. Title. II. Series.
  DS77.W34 2008
  956.704—dc22   2008016980

Chelsea House books are available at special discounts when purchased in bulk quantities for businesses, associations, institutions, or sales promotions. Please call our Special Sales Department in New York at (212) 967-8800 or (800) 322-8755.

You can find Chelsea House on the World Wide Web at
http://www.chelseahouse.com

Series design by Annie O'Donnell
Cover design by Jooyoung An

Printed in the United States of America

Bang EJB 10 9 8 7 6 5 4 3 2 1

This book is printed on acid-free paper.

All links and Web addresses were checked and verified to be correct at the time of publication. Because of the dynamic nature of the Web, some addresses and links may have changed since publication and may no longer be valid.

Contents

A New Iraq

The team of 600 American soldiers from the 4th Infantry Division and U.S. Special Forces moved carefully through the small town of al-Dawr, located in western Iraq. It was 8:00 P.M. on Saturday, December 13, 2003, and the soldiers had received a tip that the man who the U.S. military had been hunting for nearly nine months might be hiding nearby. That man was Saddam Hussein, the former ruler of Iraq, who had gone into hiding when U.S. forces had swept into Iraq's capital, Baghdad. The huge statue of Saddam erected in Baghdad had been toppled on April 9; shortly after that, the former dictator had apparently vanished. Rumors were that he was moving from one hiding place to another, traveling throughout Iraq, sometimes lingering in one spot for no more than three hours before moving to another.

Two days earlier, U.S. forces had captured a member of Saddam's inner circle, who had provided the information that Saddam might be in hiding in a rural farmhouse in al-Dawr, about nine miles from his hometown of Tikrit. The farm was owned by one of Saddam's servants and had been searched two weeks earlier. But this time, armed with more definitive information that Saddam was in the area, the search was more intense.

The soldiers broke into two groups and scoured the area, first hunting through the old farmhouse but finding nothing. They cordoned off the area and began scraping paint off walls, searching for hidden doors or tunnels.

On the property was a small, walled compound containing a mud hut and a metal lean-to, and the search continued there.

As American forces marched into Baghdad, Iraqis tore down a large statue of Saddam Hussein in the center of the city. Iraqi men swarmed the area with sledge-hammers and chisels, cheering as U.S. Marines helped pull this larger-than-life image of Saddam Hussein off its pedestal *(above)*.

The soldiers eventually uncovered what would later be described as a "spider hole," a narrow hole eight feet deep, hidden beneath a cover of dirt and bricks in front of the mud hut.

After uncovering the hole, the soldiers descended into it. There, in a space only wide enough for a single person to lie down, they found a disheveled man in rumpled clothes, with shaggy hair and a beard streaked with gray and white.

"I am Saddam Hussein, president of Iraq," the man said. "And I am willing to negotiate."

The man who had terrorized Iraq for more than 30 years, who had numerous ornate palaces scattered throughout the country, whose statue guarded the entrance to every village, and whose picture could be found in nearly every Iraqi home, was found hiding in a hole, armed only with a pistol, which he did not fire.

A jubilant L. Paul Bremer III, the United States civil administrator in Iraq, announced the news at a press conference on December 15. Speaking slowly and choosing to begin the announcement with a simple phrase that could quickly be translated so that all would understand, Bremer stated, "Ladies and gentlemen, we got him."

The press conference was held in one of Saddam's former palaces. As photos of the captured dictator were shown, his face haggard, his hair being checked for lice, many of the Iraqis in the audience cheered and wept with emotion. The man who had led his country into three devastating wars, who was responsible for the deaths of hundreds of thousands of his own people, had been reduced to a scruffy old man, being poked and prodded by a medical examiner.

For the 25 million Iraqis, the capture of Saddam Hussein marked a definite end to his rule. He had terrorized and governed for three decades; many Iraqis had known no other leader. As long as he had been in hiding, there had been the belief—the fear—that he might one day return to power. But as images of the humbled and humiliated leader flashed on the news, it was clear to all that Saddam's brutal rule over Iraq had come to an end at last.

But with the troops of the United States and a coalition of other foreign countries occupying their land, the Iraqis could not claim to be free. The end of Saddam's rule over Iraq was simply that—an ending. What precisely would begin in its place was unclear. Who would govern the country, and what form that government would take, had not yet been decided. Sunni and Shiite Muslims who had once lived side by side in relative harmony were now splintering, violently clashing in what many described as a civil war.

The British prime minister, Tony Blair, described the capture of Saddam Hussein as "very good news for the people of Iraq." The American president, George W. Bush, said, "In the history of Iraq, a dark and painful era is over. All Iraqis can now come together and reject violence and build a new Iraq." Arab newspapers printed the story of the disheveled, captured Saddam on their front pages, but their focus was on the ongoing occupation of Iraq by American troops. Their conclusion was that capture of Saddam would not cause a decrease in the violence by those resisting the American occupation, but in fact might cause it to intensify. One editorial, in the Egyptian newspaper *al-Ahram*, noted:

> This occupation will necessarily lead to resistance whether Saddam Hussein was free or detained. His arrest, however, may also encourage the Shiites who form some 60 percent of the population to join the resistance against the occupation without fearing the return of Saddam Hussein to power. It is most probable that the resistance will continue as long as there is an American-British occupation in Iraq.

It was this last statement that would prove the most prophetic. For years, the Shiite and Sunni Muslims in Iraq had been separated not only by their differing religions, based on centuries-old views of who had been the legitimate heir to the Prophet Muhammad, but on their differing roles in Iraqi society. The minority Sunnis, with their connection to Saddam and their greater numbers in Baghdad, had traditionally occupied the positions of power in Iraq's government. The Shiites had been discriminated against and largely excluded from positions of influence. But with Saddam removed from power, his strict control no longer determined which group held power. And the occupying forces did not immediately recognize the impact this would have in Iraqi society.

A LASTING LEGACY

For nearly a century, many different men and women have attempted to build a new Iraq. Their visions have involved monarchies, dictatorships, and democracies. Western nations have overseen the creation of more than one Iraqi constitution. In the early part of the twentieth century, Britain occupied the land until the cost of stamping out revolts and maintaining the peace became so expensive that the British public demanded an end to the costly occupation. In the early part of the twenty-first century, the United States found itself in a strikingly similar position.

The very name of the country—Iraq—and the decision as to where its borders would be were determined by a foreign nation. Not only did the British decide who would be defined as an Iraqi when they chose that name and determined who lived within its borders, but they decided that this new Iraq would be ruled by a monarchy and then selected a foreigner, Faisal from Arabia, to be its first king. The principal concern of the British was to create a nation in the Middle East that would be friendly to their interests.

A military coup later sought to shape a new Iraq, one that would no longer be ruled by a royal family but instead would be a republic, with an elected president, and whose official religion would be Islam. After later coups, Communists and Socialists proclaimed the need for a "new Iraq." In the late 1960s, the Ba'ath Party seized power, announcing its goal for Iraq: "One Arab Nation with an Eternal Mission," the mission being the unification of all Arab peoples and countries into a single, powerful national force. One of its members was a man named Saddam Hussein.

When Saddam seized power in 1979, his vision of a new Iraq was a country firmly under his control and a country that dominated the region. Saddam was simultaneously the president of the republic, the commander in chief of the armed forces, Iraq's field marshal, and prime minister. Saddam's power was absolute in Iraq, and through fear and force, he managed to keep tight

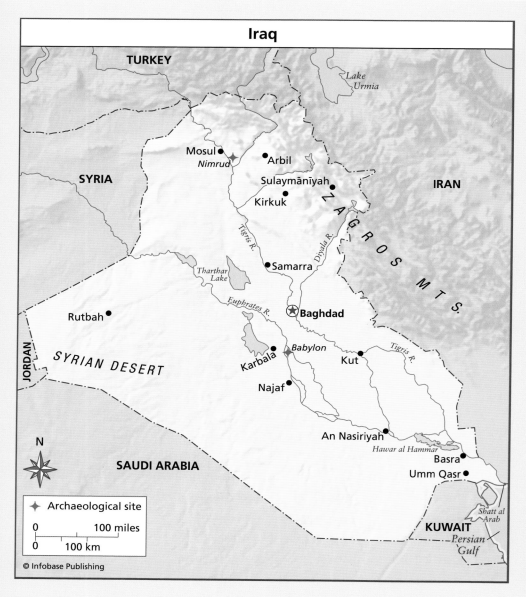

Iraq

TURKEY

Lake Urmia

Mosul
Nimrud
Arbil
Sulaymānīyah
Kirkuk

SYRIA

IRAN

Z A G R O S   M T S.

Tigris R.

Diyala R.

Tharthar Lake

Samarra

Euphrates R.

★ Baghdad

Rutbah

SYRIAN DESERT

Babylon

Karbala

Kut

Tigris R.

Najaf

JORDAN

An Nasiriyah

Hawar al Hammar

Basra

Umm Qasr

N

SAUDI ARABIA

Shatt al Arab

✦ Archaeological site

0	100 miles
0	100 km

KUWAIT

Persian Gulf

© Infobase Publishing

Bordered by the famed Tigris and Euphrates rivers, Iraq is located in the area that was formerly known as Mesopotamia, commonly referred to as the "cradle of civilization." Archaeologists believe written language, law, religion, and government were first practiced in ancient Iraq.

control of its people. His policies led Iraq into three disastrous wars—an eight-year war with Iran, an invasion of Kuwait that was repulsed by the United States and a coalition of more than 30 other nations, and the conflict that led to the U.S. invasion in 2003 and, ultimately, to Saddam's capture.

On March 17, 2003, President George W. Bush delivered a televised address in which he argued that diplomatic efforts to resolve the crisis with Iraq had failed and that military action would probably be required to overthrow Saddam Hussein. His argument was based on the belief that Saddam possessed weapons of mass destruction and had connections with international terrorists, both of which posed a security threat to the United States. Bush also spoke to the Iraqi people and promised, "We will tear down the apparatus of terror and we will help you build a new Iraq that is prosperous and free."

But in the years since American troops first entered Baghdad, that promise of a new Iraq has not yet been delivered. As the tanks of foreign armies roll through its streets, the people of Iraq face daily threats from suicide bombers. Ethnic violence erupts throughout the country. Sunni and Shiite Muslims battle for control of neighborhoods. The country whose hospitals and universities had once been the envy of their Arab neighbors now lacks the most basic necessities for daily life, including electricity, food, water, and medicine.

One hundred years ago, the nation of Iraq did not exist. The British took the land once known as Mesopotamia, united three separate provinces (Baghdad, Basra, and Mosul), and called them a nation, the nation of Iraq. From this moment of creation we can find the seeds of the conflicts that still exist in Iraq and threaten its future.

Some scholars argue that human history began in Iraq. Few traces remain of the land where the first code of laws and the first form of writing were developed. But the past offers powerful clues about the Iraq that exists today, a nation struggling to once more shape itself into a new Iraq.

2

In Search
of Ancient History

It was 5:00 A.M. and Max Mallowan was riding his horse up the slippery, muddy path to the top of the mound at Nineveh in northern Iraq. For the young British archaeologist, the day always began with the same routine: First, he made a careful study of the weather with his boss, Dr. Reginald Campbell-Thompson. It was autumn, and the rainy season and conditions were often difficult. Once they had agreed that the weather was acceptable and digging at the site could proceed, Mallowan signaled with a light to the night watchman. The watchman then lit his lamp at the top of the mound, a sign to the workers (who had to travel several miles to reach the site) that they should come to work that day. For Mallowan, the opportunity to search for buried treasure at Nineveh was exciting. Researchers had been hunting for historical records from the ancient land of the Sumerians in southern Iraq and for evidence of the civilization of the Assyrians in northern Iraq, but in that year, 1931, archaeologists were beginning to search for examples of life that dated back to prehistoric times, before written records existed. The site at Nineveh was rich with hints of a civilization that flourished before recorded time.

The contents of the enormous mound at Nineveh, Mallowan's research indicated, were three-quarters prehistoric. As the workers dug deeper and deeper, they uncovered evidence of civilizations that existed before the ancient Assyrians, though the precise dating of the bits of pottery they found was not easy.

Max Mallowan brought his wife, Agatha Christie, a mystery novelist, along with him on an archaeological dig. She later used some of her experiences at the site in her book, *Murder in Mesopotamia*, as she had witnessed many exciting events with her husband's team in the ancient city of Ur.

The beauty of this part of northern Iraq was all around them—the snow-covered Kurdish mountains, the Tigris River, and, in the distance, the gleaming minarets of the city of Mosul. Mallowan had been joined at the site by his wife, the mystery writer Agatha Christie, who had traveled from England to spend the months before Christmas by his side. One day, taking a break from the hard work, they rented a car and set off to find the site of another, much earlier, archaeological dig—at Nimrud, which had last been explored by archaeologists nearly a hundred years earlier. The rains made the roads difficult to travel, but eventually he and Agatha found the spot. It was a beautiful place a mile from the Tigris. As they picnicked at the peaceful site, giant stone Assyrian heads rising up from the ground, the remains of those earlier excavations, kept watch.

Mallowan laid out a plan for his wife: Someday they would return to this place, only he would be leading his own archaeological team rather than working as someone's assistant. They would continue the work at Nimrud that had begun a hundred years earlier, and they would, he was certain, discover great things.

THE TREASURES OF NIMRUD

It would be 20 years before Mallowan's dream would come true, but the discoveries he made at Nimrud in the 1950s were extraordinary. The ancient civilizations that had flourished in Iraq were among the world's earliest. The land had once been known as Mesopotamia, or "Land Between the Rivers," for its position between the Tigris and Euphrates rivers. It had been the home of the ancient Assyrians and the Sumerians—the land of the famed city of Babylon—and from this once-fertile territory had now come some of the world's greatest evidence of early life. Nineveh, where Mallowan had assisted Dr. Campbell-Thompson in the 1930s, had been the political capital of Assyria while Nimrud had been the military capital, and Mallowan was confident that this site still had many important secrets to reveal.

Indeed, Mallowan's instinct proved correct. Early on, the site produced valuable objects made of ivory, engraved shells containing cosmetics, and fragments of cuneiform writing (ancient writing that had wedge-shaped characters) on wax. Mallowan's team uncovered monuments indicating that the city had been completed in 879 B.C., as well as records telling of a banquet served over 10 days to 7,000 people to celebrate the occasion of the city's completion.

Many years later, Agatha Christie recalled the excitement of one day, when workers who were exploring a series of brick-lined wells rushed in shouting, "We have found a woman in the well! There is a woman in the well!" They brought in a giant mound of mud, and after gentle cleaning, an ivory head emerged bearing a smiling face surrounded with black hair that had been carefully preserved in the mud for 2,500 years. The team also found an ivory carving showing a man being attacked by a lioness amid a cluster of papyrus reeds and lotus flowers; the flowers were decorated with jewels and the man's hair gleamed with real gold. Mallowan discovered a tablet listing the military supplies at Nimrud, including a collection of 36,242 bows, most likely used by an army twice as large.

At the edge of Nimrud, the team uncovered traces of a mighty palace with 200 rooms covering nearly 12 acres. The palace had been the home of King Shalmaneser, and in one room they found the base of his throne, decorated with pictures of the highlights of his reign. The palace revealed spectacular murals, ivory carvings, sections of the rooms that once belonged to the queen, and even rooms that had housed a harem.

OTHER EXPLORERS, OTHER TREASURES

For 10 years, Mallowan and his team uncovered the wonders of an ancient city piece by piece, revealing glimpses of Iraq's history, which had only been guessed at before. Mallowan's team, however, was not the only one digging through dirt and sand to find the glories of lost worlds. Mallowan had begun his career working for the famous British archaeologist Leonard Woolley, who had led a dig at the site of the ancient Sumerian city of Ur, in southern Iraq, from 1921 to 1934. Woolley believed that, in the pale sands of the desert there, he had found the home of Abraham, who, according to the Bible, was the father of the Hebrew people. Whether the house Woolley's team uncovered belonged to the biblical Abraham or not is still being debated by archaeological researchers, but the team made many other

Archaeologists digging in Ur unearthed the tomb of the ancient Mesopotamian queen, Puabi. Surprisingly, like the resting place of Egyptian pharaoh Tutankhamen, Queen Puabi's tomb was untouched and many of her treasures were intact. One of the most extraordinary finds among her possessions was an elaborate gold headdress, which was almost a foot tall *(above)*.

amazing finds, including the remains of the petite Queen Puabi in a tomb filled with gold, jewels, statues, and musical instruments. The queen, who died at Ur nearly 600 years before Abraham was born, was buried with a large gold headpiece that measured nearly a foot high. Her tomb also held the remains of 21 servants who were killed or killed themselves in order to be with her in death.

Woolley's discoveries at Ur told scholars much about the history and culture of ancient Sumeria. They also provide glimpses of the Middle East we know today, including such familiar elements as streets lined with open booths, much like the modern bazaars. The first written evidence of the existence of medical doctors was discovered on a tablet at Ur dating back to 2700 B.C. It is in the splendor of the tombs and palaces, however, that the vastness of this once-mighty civilization was most clearly revealed.

The promise of ancient wealth and rich treasures lured many invading armies to conquer this territory throughout history and brought many archaeological explorers to the area in the early part of the twentieth century. It was believed by some that the Garden of Eden could be found here. In the ancient cuneiform inscriptions could be found some of the earliest examples of written language. The legends of the Tower of Babel, the Hanging Gardens of Babylon, and the empire of King Nebuchadnezzar captured the imagination of these scientific explorers, and the cuneiform writings and records they uncovered told of the ancient Assyrians and Sumerians and the wondrous civilization they built that flourished in the Middle East for 2,000 years before slipping into the sand. The British, the French, the Germans, and the Americans all sent teams into what is now Iraq, and the treasures they discovered fill museums around the world today.

But while these discoveries showed the glories of the civilizations that had peopled the land in ancient times, the country that we know today as Iraq began taking shape only in the years following World War I. The land once known as the center of world civilization and culture, where so much of recorded ancient history took place, is now recognized mainly as a land ripped apart by war and conflict.

What happened to this place, located at the eastern edge of the Arab world, to shape its modern history? How did a land that produced the earliest forms of writing and the first code of laws became a country in ruins, devastated by violence?

While Leonard Woolley, Max Mallowan, and others were digging through the earth for evidence of the ancient history of Iraq, a brand-new nation was taking shape around them.

A Nation Is Created

Many of the countries of the Middle East that we know today—such as Saudi Arabia, Israel, or Iraq—could not be found on a map before World War I. The land was there, of course, and the people as well, but the names with which we identify specific people and places in that part of the world today were not used more than a hundred years ago. If you look at a map of the region drawn at the very beginning of the twentieth century, you will find some unfamiliar names and unusual boundaries defining countries much larger than those on a modern map.

In the ancient Middle East, conquering armies charged in and snatched up immense expanses of land, building empires that lasted for centuries before being swept away by the next set of conquerors. Maps from the early 1900s reveal this history. The region was divided into huge sections, marked by names like Turkestan, Persia, and Mesopotamia, that stretched from the Mediterranean Sea to the Indian subcontinent in vast, empty expanses with few additional markings for cities or smaller territories.

For a thousand years, the land now known as Iraq had been conquered by a series of fierce warriors on horseback, who came from central and northeast Asia and seized the terrain over which they traveled as they headed west. The Ottomans took the territories of modern Iraq in about A.D. 1500. Speakers of the Turkish language and followers of the Islamic faith, these conquerors at one time held within their empire most of the Middle East, northern Africa, and parts of Europe. At the beginning of the twentieth century, the region we now know as Iraq was still part of the Ottoman Empire.

The empire's economic growth depended on slave labor and on its ability to continue to invade new lands, seize goods, and capture new slaves, as well as to expand the market for trade in Ottoman goods. But it became increasingly difficult for the empire's leaders to govern so many different peoples, keep so many territories under control, and ensure that orders were followed while also continuing to conquer new regions. Expanding Russian and British empires added to the challenge, making it harder for the Ottomans to rule their lands.

The Ottoman Empire was a Muslim state, yet even within that simple framework, differences emerged. Nearly half of all Ottoman subjects were Christians or Jews. And within the empire two groups, or sects, of Muslims existed. The Sunnis represented the largest number of Muslims within the empire. They regarded the Ottoman leaders as spiritual guides and the successors to the Prophet Muhammad. The Shiites disagreed with many of the Ottoman policies and did not support the Ottoman claim to be the rightful spiritual and religious leaders of the people they ruled.

So, as the winds of war slowly swept over the globe at the beginning of the twentieth century, drawing nation after nation into the conflict that became World War I, the empire the Ottomans had built in the Middle East was crumbling. Young, ambitious political leaders in Turkey seized power and attempted to launch reforms to hold the territory together. But it was too little, too late. Other powers and other nations had moved into the region, recognizing the opportunities the weakened Ottoman Empire presented and sensing the wealth that lay beneath the desert sand. Just a short time earlier, the great powers of Europe had carved up Africa. Now they turned their eyes to the Middle East. The British, the French, the Germans, and the Russians all were viewed with trepidation by the last of the Ottoman leadership.

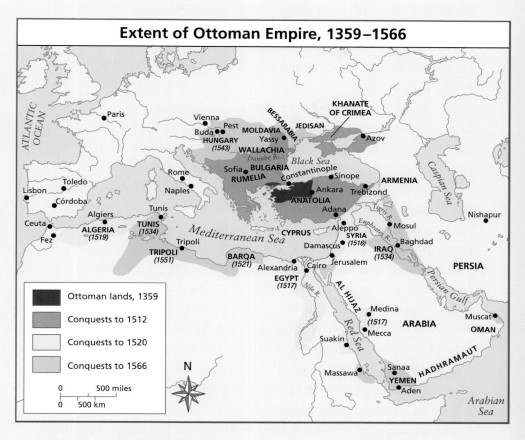

Extent of Ottoman Empire, 1359–1566

Legend:
- Ottoman lands, 1359
- Conquests to 1512
- Conquests to 1520
- Conquests to 1566

0 500 miles
0 500 km

N

Map labels: ATLANTIC OCEAN, Paris, Vienna, Pest, Buda, HUNGARY (1543), MOLDAVIA, Yassy, BESSARABIA, JEDISAN, KHANATE OF CRIMEA, Azov, WALLACHIA, Danube R., Black Sea, Rome, Sofia, BULGARIA, RUMELIA, Constantinople, Sinope, ARMENIA, Caspian Sea, Toledo, Lisbon, Córdoba, Naples, Ankara, Trebizond, ANATOLIA, Adana, Nishapur, Algiers, Tunis, Ceuta, ALGERIA (1519), TUNIS (1534), Fez, Tripoli, Mediterranean Sea, CYPRUS, Aleppo, SYRIA (1516), Mosul, Euphrates R., Tigris R., Baghdad, Damascus, IRAQ (1534), PERSIA, TRIPOLI (1551), BARQA (1521), Alexandria, Cairo, Jerusalem, EGYPT (1517), Nile R., AL HIJAZ, Medina (1517), Muscat, OMAN, ARABIA, Mecca, Suakin, Red Sea, HADHRAMAUT, Massawa, Sanaa, YEMEN, Aden, Arabian Sea, Persian Gulf

The Ottoman Empire was spread throughout areas of the Middle East, Africa, Central Asia, and Eastern Europe. Its rule over these regions caused deep conflicts and differences that continue to exist in modern times. Groups like the Sunni and Shiite Muslims in Iraq, for example, are set against each other based on rifts that began during the Ottoman reign.

A REMARKABLE WOMAN

When you think of the powerful leaders whose words and actions shaped the modern history of Iraq, you may picture nomadic tribesmen in traditional desert robes or prime ministers and statesmen from the various parts of Europe, building railroads and trade routes leading them deep into the territories of the Middle East. You may imagine the military men whose campaigns brought them fame and resulted in expansion of the lands controlled by their nations. But it was a woman named Gertrude Bell who actually shaped the destiny of the land that today we call Iraq.

A courageous and accomplished British traveler, Bell was described by some as the "Desert Queen." Through her letters and books, she painted a picture of the Mesopotamian region that showed, in truer colors than ever before, the vastness and richness of the land and its people. Her words influenced the British statesmen who became her friends, and her thoughts and ideas greatly contributed to the establishment of the borders and government that shape Iraq even to this day.

Gertrude Bell was born on July 14, 1868, in Durham, England, to a wealthy family. Her mother died when she was only three years old. Her father, a highly educated and successful man, encouraged his daughter's curiosity and sent her away to school in London when she was 15. This was an unusual step in the late 1800s, when most of the girls of Gertrude's social class and background were educated at home by tutors and then, when they reached the age of 17, were presented to society. The goal for girls of that time was to find a good husband, and they were expected to marry before they turned 20.

But Gertrude's father was a more progressive thinker. He recognized Gertrude's intelligence and encouraged her to use her mind. She was an excellent student and, at 18, she decided to attend Oxford University. In 1886, when Bell first entered Oxford, the presence of women in the classroom was rare. In fact, in the university's 700-year history to that point, women had been allowed to attend for only the seven years prior to Bell's arrival there. And although they were allowed to attend the lectures, the handful of young women students were expected to sit separately from the young men, sometimes on the same raised platform from which the professor lectured, placing them directly in front of the curious and unfriendly eyes of the male

British writer and government official Gertrude Bell (1868–1926) held a deep love for the Middle East. Her knowledge of the Arabian Peninsula led her into service with British intelligence during World War I and she was influential in British policy toward Iraqi independence and in the selection of Faisal as Iraq's first king.

students. One history professor allowed Bell in his class only if she sat in the room with her back to him! Despite these obstacles, Bell performed brilliantly and earned the highest mark (called a First) in Modern History. She was the first woman to do so, an accomplishment so newsworthy that it was published in the London *Times*.

But for young women of that Victorian era, educational accomplishments meant little—the most important goal was to marry. By the time she was 23, Bell was still unmarried and feeling quite lonely. When her aunt invited her to join her on a trip to Persia (a region that we know today as Iran), Bell spent several months studying the language and familiarizing herself with the customs of the people. In the spring of 1892, she set out from the cold gray of England, boarded the Orient Express from Paris to Constantinople, and then traveled by boat to Persia. The young woman who left England that spring and emerged into the dazzling colors of the Middle East was soon to become a transformed person. In a letter to her cousin written two months after her arrival, she said, "Are we the same people, I wonder, when all our surroundings, associations, acquaintances are changed?" The Middle East would shape Gertrude Bell's destiny, just as clearly as she shaped its own.

ARABIAN ADVENTURES

That first trip to Persia sparked a new life for Bell. Although she returned from time to time to visit family in England, she found an excitement in the Middle East that made life at home seem dull and drab. She enjoyed great freedom in the new lands she explored; the rules and customs that governed a woman's behavior in strict Victorian England had little meaning in the desert.

Her study habits served her well. Unlike many travelers to foreign countries, she made a point of learning the customs and the languages of the places she visited. She learned to carry on a conversation in French, Italian, German, Persian, Turkish, and Arabic, and these skills (acquired only after years of study) made it possible for her to live comfortably among the people she encountered on her travels. She quickly moved beyond the places well traveled by tourists and often headed out on horseback to the desert, accompanied by a few native guides. There, she encountered tribesmen and nomads who, suspicious of the British woman at first, grew to accept and even trust her as they shared confidences in their native language over cups of strong Turkish coffee.

Bell learned much about the local politics as she traveled through the crumbling Ottoman territories. She returned to England to write a book that contained descriptions and photographs of what she had seen in the Middle East. It was immediately successful, and it marked her as an expert in the culture of the Middle East. Other books and articles would follow.

Bell decided to acquire a new set of skills while she was in England. She learned surveying, how to chart position and direction based on the stars, and some basic techniques for mapmaking. She returned to the Middle East, this time with a new goal: She would visit Mesopotamia and create maps of the uncharted deserts there.

Her travels took her into unfamiliar and often dangerous regions. War had broken out among some of the desert tribes, and she was captured and held prisoner for 10 days by one wealthy tribal leader. Water and food supplies frequently ran low. And yet Bell journeyed on, photographing and taking notes for the books and articles that would open up the mysteries of Mesopotamia to British readers.

Among those who followed her adventures with great interest were British politicians, who recognized the opportunities the collapsing Ottoman Empire held. By 1908, Constantinople, the capital of the Ottoman Empire, was in chaos. A group of students from the universities and military academies there, who became known as the Young Turks, had forced the sultan to abdicate and had taken over the government. But the new government they formed faced financial problems, and they were eager to borrow money and aid from the Europeans, who were happy to oblige in return for firming up their position in the region.

Germany was particularly interested in the area and had a good relationship with the Young Turks, because the majority of the military academies many of them had attended were run by German officers. At the beginning of the twentieth century, Germany was also constructing a strategic railroad line to run from Berlin to Baghdad. This railroad threatened the security of the British, who worried about the increasing German presence in a region that was important in part because it lay along the route to India, the "crown jewel" in the British Empire at the time.

In addition, by 1911 the British navy was switching its mighty battleships from coal-burning engines to oil, making it possible for them to travel farther and faster and be refueled at sea. While Great Britain had plenty of coal, it had no oil, and it was eager to find a steady supply in the Middle East.

Thus, Bell's knowledge of the region and her familiarity with the local politics and important players made her a great resource to British leaders. Ambassadors and foreign secretaries relied on her information, and as the conflict that broke out in Sarajevo (Yugoslavia) in 1914 quickly engulfed Europe in what would become known as World War I, Great Britain's need for precious Middle East oil became even more urgent. In late 1915, Bell was asked by British military intelligence to go to Cairo, Egypt, to help with the war effort by providing valuable insight into the impact the war was having on the Middle East.

After a few months in Egypt, Bell was sent on to the region of Mesopotamia to collect information from the Arabs and to share what she learned with the British intelligence service.

FROM SPY TO KINGMAKER

The information Bell gathered was equally useful after World War I ended. Great Britain occupied Mesopotamia, but British politicians held deeply divided opinions about how best to handle this new territory. Sir Arnold Wilson, the British officer responsible for managing the region from 1918 to 1920, felt that the territory should become a British protectorate, linked to India and governed by Indian immigrants who had bravely served the British Empire during the war. But Bell, who was by then working for Sir Arnold, felt differently, and she and others in the region argued equally strongly that the region should be governed by Arabs.

It quickly became clear that while British popular opinion supported many different options, there was one point of agreement: The former Ottoman provinces in the region needed a new system of government.

Local trouble began not long after World War I ended, when the League of Nations began carving up the former Ottoman Empire, officially giving different portions to the victorious Allied forces. At the San Remo Conference of April 25, 1920, Prime Minister Lloyd George of Great Britain and Premier Georges Clemenceau of France reached an agreement on how to divide the Arab region: Arabia would remain independent; Syria (including Lebanon) would be mandated to the French; and Mesopotamia and Palestine would be mandated to the British. While the French agreed to grant Mosul in northern Mesopotamia to the British, it was only with the understanding that both France and Britain would share in oil exploration and production there.

With this meeting, the fate of the Middle East was seemingly decided without Arabic participation or consultation. When the news reached the people of Mesopotamia, they were outraged. In June 1920, a sheikh who had been imprisoned by the British for refusing to pay a debt launched a revolt that spread throughout the tribal areas near the Euphrates River and on to the regions north and east of Baghdad, destroying railroad tracks and bridges in the process. The British brought in the Royal Air Force to bomb the troubled areas. By the time the revolt ended, 400 British had been killed and £40 million (British pounds) had been spent to bring the region back under control. To the British public, it was a ridiculous waste of lives and money. The outcry was clear: It was time to pull back from the region, and British politicians began to look for a leader with an Arab background but who would still be friendly to British interests.

In October 1920, Sir Percy Cox returned to the region as the British government's high commissioner. Sir Percy had lived for many years in Arab countries, and he was respected for his sensitivity to Arab sentiments as well as for his political skills. It was during the celebration to herald Sir Percy's return that the name *Iraq* was first used officially by the British. (The word means "well-rooted" or "having ancient roots" in Arabic and had been used by medieval Muslims to refer to parts of Mesopotamia.) On that date, October 11, 1920, Sir Percy promised that Iraq would belong to and be ruled by the Arabic people. He then immediately set to work to make his promise a reality as well as ensuring that Great Britain would retain the strategic and economic advantages it required in the region.

Gertrude Bell supported Sir Percy's position on Arabic rule. Her contacts among a wide range of Iraqi people made her invaluable as the search began for an appropriate leader. Gertrude met with tribesmen and townsmen, military and religious leaders, all in an effort to find out who might most easily win public support and avoid another disastrous revolt.

In the end, it was a foreigner who was chosen as the future king of Iraq. Faisal had recently lost his throne in Syria when he was sent into exile by the French. A quiet, serious man, Faisal had been the middle son in a powerful Saudi Arabian political family, and his rise to the throne of Iraq would spark great envy in his brothers. He was a controversial choice—the language he spoke was different from the Arabic of the Iraqi people he would need to govern; he was from Mecca (in Arabia), not Iraq; and he clearly had strong ties to the British. Nevertheless, the British were committed to pulling back from their involvement in the region and needed a local leader to quiet the complaints of both the people of Iraq, who resented the British presence in their

In 1921, a group considered to be experts on the Middle East met in Cairo to decide the fate of Iraq. Both Gertrude Bell *(second row, 2nd from left)*, T.E. Lawrence *(second row, 4th from right)*, and future British prime minister Winston Churchill *(seated, 4th from left)* helped this group create the borders and governing body of the new Iraq.

homeland, and the people back in England, who resented the cost of the Middle East efforts.

So in March 1921, a group of representatives gathered in Cairo to decide the future of Iraq. Winston Churchill, at the time an official with the British colonial secretary, described the group as "Forty Thieves," although they really numbered 38. They were considered to be the leading experts on the Middle

East, and Gertrude Bell was among them. During this conference, representatives sketched out the boundaries of what would become the kingdom of Iraq. They agreed on the appointment of Faisal as king, and they discussed the best ways to ensure that he would be accepted by the Iraqi people.

It was agreed that Faisal's suitability as king depended on his acceptability to the people on both religious as well as political grounds. As a member of the royal Sharifian family, Faisal was a descendent of the Prophet Muhammad, the central religious figure in Islam. To emphasize this connection, the Cairo Conference agreed that Faisal would need to go to Mecca, the birthplace of the Prophet Muhammad and considered the holiest of all places in Islam. From there, he would travel to Iraq, as if he had been summoned by the Iraqi people to lead them on a pilgrimage to power, providing them with both a spiritual and political leadership that had been lacking under the British.

The challenges that faced Faisal were overwhelming. He was a Sunni Muslim, ruling a country in which the majority of the people were Shiite. The provinces that had been divided by the Ottomans into different territories (Baghdad, Basra, and Mosul) and that were now to be united as part of his kingdom varied greatly in their religious and ethnic communities. In the north lay Kurdistan, a region whose people spoke a different language altogether (Kurdish) and considered themselves to be more closely connected to other Kurdish people in Turkey than to the Iraqi people who were now their countrymen. The cities of the new kingdom contained large populations of Christians and Jews. For Faisal, the task was enormous: He would be a new king in a new nation, trying to gather up the strands of an empire the British found too expensive to govern.

At the time of his coronation, on August 23, 1921, Faisal was 36 years old. A new flag was raised over the new nation, and a proclamation declared that 96 percent of the people of Mesopotamia had elected him king. The British were relieved at this solution to their problems. They felt confident that they could continue to influence the direction of the country while allow-ing it to be governed by Arabs.

Gertrude Bell was among the most enthusiastic supporters of Faisal. She made a great effort to educate him in the wonders of his new kingdom, inviting archaeologists to lecture on the treasures of the digs and providing his staff with instructions about the ceremonies that should play a part in the life of the court. Neither she nor her British countrymen fully understood that Faisal and the Iraqi people had no intention of being guided through the process of governing their own country. They wished to shape their own destiny, and the route they intended to take required complete independence.

Although it was not clear in the beginning, the British influ-ence on Iraq was waning. Gertrude Bell was an early casualty. Having been involved so closely in the beginning, shaping Iraq's destiny from the largest scale (helping to decide where the boundaries of the new country would be drawn) to the smaller details (deciding on an appropriate design for the new nation's flag), Bell found her role greatly diminished in the new monar-chy. She became involved in establishing a museum to safeguard the antiquities emerging from Iraq's archaeological sites, but the excitement and intrigue she had enjoyed as a source of critical information for the British and Arabs alike was gone. She was ill suited to a quiet life of garden parties and picnics and became depressed by the downturn in her own usefulness and by her family's economic struggles after the war. On July 11, 1926, she took her own life. The king that she had helped bring to power would outlive her by only seven years.

4

Independence and Its Consequences

Before becoming king, Faisal was a respected military leader. He had led an Arab army in battles against the Ottomans, and his ability to unite many different forces under a single banner of Arab unity served him well in his early days of ruling Iraq. The people were deeply divided into three groups. There were those who felt a loyalty to the British and wished to continue the mandate granting Great Britain 20 years to oversee Iraq. There were others who wished for independence and full Arab control. And there were those who still felt greater ties to the old Ottoman Empire and wished to reestablish a connection with Turkey. King Faisal expertly balanced these conflicting demands and moved smoothly among the differing factions, seeming to agree with each group yet, at the same time, steadily moving Iraq in the direction he felt was best.

But the clique with which Faisal felt most comfortable consisted of other military officers who shared many of the same experiences: Ottoman military training, similar schooling, and a Sunni perspective on religion. One of his close advisers was Nuri as-Said, a military officer who had first served in the Turkish army and then later followed Faisal's leadership into the Arab army that revolted against Ottoman rule.

Nuri as-Said was born in Baghdad in 1888, and so offered the king an adviser who was also a native of the region. He ultimately became prime minister of Iraq in 1930. In that position,

King Faisal *(above)*, the first leader and ruler of Iraq, delicately handled the differences that threatened to split his country into factions. Communities throughout the region, while nationalistic, were also fiercely proud of their own ethnicities, religious views, and independence. King Faisal learned how to draw out their support and manage their rifts.

he was faced with the challenge of negotiating a new treaty with the British.

RUMBLINGS OF INDEPENDENCE

The first treaty with Great Britain had been signed shortly after Faisal was crowned king. As a formal documentation of the relationship between Iraq and Great Britain, the treaty was to make clear that the terms of the mandate put into place by the League of Nations would largely be left in place by the new Iraqi government. Iraq agreed to cooperate with the League of Nations, to respect religious freedom, to allow missionaries to continue their work, to respect the rights of foreigners, and to treat all nations equally. The agreement stated that Great Britain would be consulted on foreign and domestic matters, including military efforts, judicial decisions, and financial concerns. In return, Great Britain agreed to prepare Iraq for membership in the League of Nations, although the time frame for this was extremely vague. The treaty, signed on October 10, 1922, was meant to last for 20 years.

But as time passed, Faisal felt strongly that the 20-year period of British oversight was far too long. This was not the kingdom he intended to rule—a kingdom essentially operating under the scrutiny of a British microscope. And the British public was equally displeased. There had been a movement in England to reduce expenses in Iraq drastically. The people wanted an assurance that this would happen quickly, not over a 20-year period. So, less than a year later, on April 30, 1923, the treaty was changed, shortening the period of time that Great Britain would oversee Iraq to four years.

The next step was for Iraq to draw up its own constitution. Finally drafted, adopted, and signed by the king in March 1925, the new constitution specified that Iraq would be ruled by a monarchy, that the government would follow a parliamentary format, and that the legislature would consist of two parts—an elected house of representatives and an appointed senate.

The system of government chosen was similar in nature to that of Great Britain, and it made it possible for the British to continue to operate behind the scenes, dictating policy and influencing decision making. And despite the fact that there was an elected group of representatives, the king held the power to call for new elections whenever he wanted and to create or dismiss cabinets and prime ministers at will. As a result, the king held a great deal of power over all the elected officials. If a member of his cabinet became too powerful, the king would dismiss him. Because there was a limited number of politicians in Iraq that had the necessary experience, the king frequently hired and fired the same people several times over.

Nuri as-Said is one example of this revolving door; he served as prime minister 14 different times. Between 1920 and 1936, there were 21 different cabinets, and only 27 people held the top positions. In that group, there were 14 men making the key decisions while constantly moving in and out of office, changing jobs, being fired and rehired at the king's whim.

Chaos was inevitable. Rumblings had begun among the Iraqi people that full independence was the only way for Iraq to take its rightful place in the Arab world. Revolts continued on small scales throughout the country. As the British army began to pull out of the farthest stretches of the country, those responsible for the revolts became bolder in their cries against the British. Different parts of the country were pulling away from the center.

Faisal and others in his government felt that Iraq could never fully develop, either politically or economically, while it was still necessary to check any and all major decisions with Great Britain. He and other political officers, who had been trained in German military schools in the old days of the Ottoman Empire, had been greatly impressed by the German emphasis on nationalism and pride in one's country. German history contained similar experiences of uniting diverse groups under a single banner of national pride, and Faisal took those lessons seriously. It seemed clear that Iraq must be able to govern itself without a foreign power overseeing its efforts.

In response to the demands of the British and Iraqi people, the British government eventually agreed to end what had become an unworkable system. Nuri as-Said, serving then in one of his many stints as prime minister, worked hard to develop a more sensible agreement with Great Britain, and in 1929, Great Britain agreed to sponsor Iraq for admission into the League of Nations as a first step toward independence. But the new agreement still left a significant portion of foreign policy decision making in British hands. And while the British agreed to provide aid, equipment, and training to the Iraqi armed forces, they were also allowed to use all Iraqi railroads, airports, and seaports in the event of war. In addition, both Iraq and Great Britain agreed to take the same defensive position in the event of war—in other words, if war was declared, they would fight on the same side. The treaty was ratified in June 1930, at a time when Iraq's focus was much more on national than international worries. The prospect of war seemed far away.

A POWER STRUGGLE

On October 3, 1932, Iraq was admitted to the League of Nations as an independent state. Nuri as-Said had played an important role in leading Iraq into the League—too important, perhaps— at least in the king's eyes. Always suspicious of anyone whose power might challenge his own, King Faisal decided that as-Said must go. Upon his return from Geneva and the triumph of seeing Iraq admitted into the League of Nations, as-Said received a telegram from the king. The message: He had been fired.

Having begun the process of removing British influence from his government (by both removing Nuri as-Said and achieving independence for his country), King Faisal turned his attention to unifying all the different political groups. Those who had once passionately argued against Faisal's government, claiming that he was too dependent on the British, could now be drawn in. The king invited Rashid Ali al-Gaylani, a leader of one of the opposition movements that had struggled against him, to become prime minister in the new government. And, true to the nature of Iraqi politics, Nuri as-Said (a political opponent of Rashid Ali) was soon back, too, this time as foreign minister.

Not everyone was pleased at the exit of the British from Iraqi politics. The Assyrians, a small Christian community living in the north of Iraq, in Mosul, had been brought into Iraq during World War I to help fight with British troops, and after the war had received guarantees of protection by the British. Thus, as the British began to leave the country, the Assyrians became increasingly nervous. They asked for a firm pledge of protection from the new government, and, to create a greater level of security, Assyrians living in Syria moved back across the Iraqi border to Mosul, forming an even larger Assyrian community in the region.

The Assyrians were known to be anti-Arab and pro-British. What's more, they had served principally in the military, and rumors swirled among the Iraqis that they still were heavily armed. During British occupation, the Assyrians had been paid a higher wage than Iraqi troops. And even after independence, the Assyrians (under British protection) had not become Iraqi citizens, but instead maintained their small territory of independent people who were still much more loyal to Great Britain than to Iraq.

Trouble was clearly brewing in the north during that summer of 1933, while King Faisal was in Europe. In his absence, the new government and the newly created army decided to show their strength and prove to the Iraqi people that the days of British influence were over. Troops were sent to the northern region and several hundred Assyrians were brutally killed.

The League of Nations quickly responded to this massacre —less than a year after Iraq had signed a pledge to respect the rights of minority groups living within its borders. King Faisal rushed back to Baghdad, but it was too late. Great support had developed for the army's actions, and for conscription—a draft—requiring young men to serve a fixed term in the army unless they were the chief wage earners for their families. Within three years, the size of the army doubled.

Troops returned from the Assyrian attack in the north to victory parades. The majority of the Iraqi people were pleased with the way the army and its military officers had dealt with trouble and, at the same time, wiped out a bit more of British power in the region. As the troops marched back home, they were greeted by enthusiastic cheers for them and for their leader. But the leader receiving the applause was not Faisal; it was his son, Ghazi. When Faisal realized he could not control the situation within his own country, and suffering from heart trouble, he left for Switzerland, where he died in September 1933.

WEAK KING IN A VIOLENT TIME

Ghazi was only 21 years old when he became king. His youth and inexperience placed him at a real disadvantage when faced with the crafty maneuverings of the politicians operating in Iraq. Having moved in and out of power so frequently during King Faisal's reign, people like Nuri as-Said and others were used to forming and breaking alliances, depending on what served them best. They quickly moved in to whisper advice to the young king, most of which resulted in decisions that benefited only the whisperer.

Ghazi had supported the army's efforts against the Assyrians and encouraged the draft. The army became increasingly powerful. It also began to play a political role as Ghazi used it to stamp out any disturbances in his country and make sure that no other rebellions sprang up in the far reaches of the land. Support of the army also became an important factor in politicians' success. Generally, this required bribes and offers of better housing or fine wines and food. If politicians chose not to go along, it became increasingly difficult for them to govern and win elections. Local revolts, riots, and looting would be ignored by troops asked to restore peace. In short, the politicians needed the army much more than the army needed the politicians—a dangerous situation in a country where the king was weak and the nation was new.

Ghazi made matters worse by constantly consulting military officers on everything, even nonmilitary decisions. Thus the stage was set for the military to completely overthrow the government in power. In 1936, Hikmat Sulayman and a group of old politicians joined forces with a band of young men who supported Socialism and democracy and who wanted reforms.

This strange set of allies then urged the army to attack Baghdad. It did, and the cabinet was forced to resign. Hikmat Sulayman became the new prime minister, and he chose as his chief of staff a commander of a division of the army, thus giving the military direct influence over policy. This fact did not bring stability to the government, however, and from 1936 to 1941, as different army officers supported different politicians, government leadership changed eight different times.

Pictured are King Faisal II *(center)* with his nanny and Nuri as-Said, the prime minister of Iraq, in 1940. Faisal II became king at just four years old, during a turbulent time in Iraq after his father, King Ghazi, was killed in a car accident. His uncle Abd al-Ilah was appointed regent until Faisal reached the age of 18 and could rule on his own.

The turmoil was only beginning. In April 1939, King Ghazi, who loved fast cars, was killed in an automobile accident. His son, Faisal II, became the new king, faced with a country fraught with problems and a government in a constant state of chaos. The international picture was no brighter—World War II was about to break out.

It all would have been a nearly impossible job for the most experienced of rulers, but the new king could hardly be described as experienced. Faisal II, Iraq's new monarch, was only four years old.

5

The Forces of War

While the young Faisal II held the title of king, his actual duties were carried out by his uncle, Emir Abd al-Ilah, who had been appointed regent. This meant that al-Ilah would hold this position until Faisal II was old enough to rule on his own (considered to be when he reached the age of 18). Abd al-Ilah was strongly pro-British, a dangerous position in a country veering violently toward nationalism and away from the tradition of British involvement in the region.

Iraq's past and future collided with the outbreak of World War II in 1939. At this time, Nuri as-Said was back in power in one of his many turns as prime minister. In keeping with the 1930 agreement as-Said helped to negotiate with Great Britain, which stated that, in the event of war, Britain and Iraq would take the same defensive position, as-Said was prepared to declare war on Germany. But the powerful Iraqi army felt differently. Since some of the older officers had been trained in military schools operated by Germans during the Ottoman Empire, they sympathized with the motivation behind the Nazis' military actions and were able to overlook the racist aspects of Nazism that were most unflattering to Arabs. (Nazi anti-Semitism was not directed only at Jewish people, but at all "Semites," or descendants of those who had inhabited the ancient Middle East, including Arabs.) Ultimately, the officers allowed as-Said to break off diplomatic relations with Germany in September 1939, as the British had requested, but they refused to allow him to declare war on Germany or to send Iraqi troops to the Balkans to join in the Allied efforts there.

By the time Italy entered the war in June 1940, the Iraqi government had changed yet again. Nuri as-Said was out as prime minister, although he held the important position of minister of foreign affairs. The new prime minister was Rashid Ali al-Gaylani. The king's uncle, Abd al-Ilah, fled the country. Impressed by German victories in Holland, Denmark, and Norway, and the defeat of France, the new leaders were even more certain that if they wanted to be on the winning side, they should not link themselves with Great Britain. At this same time, there was a renewed interest among many members of the Iraqi public in creating a kind of "brotherhood of nations" among all Arab countries. The nationalists in the Iraqi government felt that their ties to their fellow Arabs should be of greater importance than any ties to countries far away in Europe. Both Syria and Palestine were under foreign control, and the Pan-Arab nationalists, as they were called, felt that the first priority should be supporting the efforts of these neighboring countries to achieve independence rather than the military campaigns being waged by countries much farther away.

The influence of the military officers, many of whom were pro-Germany, and the Pan-Arabs in positions of political power made it impossible for Rashid Ali al-Gaylani to support the British in their war effort. But some in the government went even further: They secretly approached the Germans in an effort to form a new alliance, this time with the side fighting against the Allies.

The British were concerned at the unexpected developments in the Middle East. Apart from a very small military presence stationed on the ground in Iraq to guard British air bases, the majority of British troops in place in the region were air force personnel, not ground troops. They had depended on the Iraqi force of 46,000 troops plus 12,000 police and many former military men to back up the British presence. The news that these troops now might actually be moving toward the German side was particularly unwelcome at a time when Great Britain was desperately fighting in Europe, especially given the strategic importance of access to Iraq's oil and the British air bases in Iraq.

The British decided to send troops to Basra, a large city in southern Iraq where they had built a big, modern port during World War I. Strategically, Basra was an important point from which to launch campaigns and carry supplies by sea, railway, or air—it was also close to Iran and to several of the Arabian peninsula states.

For most Iraqis, the arrival of British troops was an alarming sight. Only recently had independence been achieved; they had no interest in reverting back to the days of British occupation. Rashid Ali al-Gaylani immediately informed the British that they must move their troops out of Iraq to Palestine and that no more British troops could arrive until the first group had left the country. Great Britain refused and, instead, began sending additional troops to the military base at Habbaniya, 55 miles west of Baghdad.

At the prospect of a large British military presence so close to the country's capital, military officials in the Iraqi government decided to take the drastic step of sending their own troops into the region to guard the base and prevent additional British troops from landing. Based on their secret negotiations with the Germans, the Iraqi military felt confident that the Germans would come to their aid should the conflict turn into a war. The small numbers of British troops currently in place also made the Iraqis feel confident of victory.

The British had had enough of Iraqi resistance. On May 2, 1941, they attacked without warning, firing missiles at and shelling the Iraqi troops around their base at Habbaniya. The Iraqis fought back. The former allies were now at war.

THE BRITISH BACK IN POWER

While the Iraqis initially held the manpower advantage at Habbaniya, the British were quick to send in additional troops from other parts of the Middle East. After four short weeks, British

At the start of World War II, the British desperately needed to hold certain Middle-Eastern territories for offensive and defensive reasons. Many Iraqis, however, felt an affinity for the German side and a deep resentment toward the British. Tensions escalated, and the British invaded and occupied all of Iraq with the help of one of their regiments, the Arab Legion (above).

troops marched toward Baghdad. Iraqi leaders, including Nuri as-Said and Rashid Ali al-Gaylani, fled the country, many heading for Iran. The few who were left promptly surrendered.

Faisal II's uncle was restored to power as regent. With a friendly ruler once more in place, a pro-British government was swiftly set up. The country declared war on Germany in January 1942, and the British promptly took advantage of Iraq's bases to reinforce their military presence in the Middle East.

During the war, martial law was in effect; restrictions were put in place to limit freedom of speech (evidence that the majority of Iraqis were anti-British), inflation was high, and food shortages were frequent. After the war, the public expected these limitations to disappear. When they did not, public outcry was immediate.

In 1945, the king's uncle, still serving as regent, took a step to address some of the public's concerns. He felt that the country's parliamentary system needed to be strengthened, to give the people a sense that they were actively involved in their government. He called for the formation of political parties. It is perhaps not surprising that each political party that was formed appealed to a different group of people. Pan-Arabs spoke out strongly against the British presence in the country. The moderates supported limited reforms. Various Socialist parties supported redistributing state-owned and privately owned land, improving working conditions for the poor, and increasing access to medical care and education.

In this mix of new ideas and calls for reform, the older politicians, who wanted to hold on to their power, land, and wealth, were ill at ease. But once the calls for reform began, it was difficult to quiet them. The government that had been formed after the war in January 1946 lasted only a few short months, and then once more Nuri as-Said was back in power as prime minister. He tried to appeal to the various political parties and win their support, but he was unsuccessful. Another round of elections was called, and the political parties refused to participate, claiming that they would not be allowed to join in the political process fairly. By March 1947, as-Said had resigned and a new prime minister, the first Shiite politician to rise to that high a position, had been elected. Salih Jabr tried to hold together the many conflicting demands of his countrymen, but the biggest challenge he undertook—negotiating a new treaty with the British in the aftermath of World War II—ultimately cost him his job.

Traveling to London, Jabr met with the British to carve out the terms of a new agreement. The British had been burned once before, however, and did not wish to make the same mistakes again. They hoped to retain control of their air bases in Iraq; Jabr insisted that these must be controlled by Iraqis. After some brief negotiation, it was agreed that Iraq would regain control of the air bases—Great Britain could only use them if Iraq agreed. In addition, the British forces would leave the country, and the Iraqi army would be given both training and weapons.

Confident that he had concluded an agreement that would win great support from his people, Jabr signed the 20-year treaty in January 1948. But he had not correctly understood how strong the anti-British sentiment had grown in his country. As news of the treaty's terms reached Iraq, riots broke out in Baghdad.

With Jabr still in London, the king's uncle called in both older and younger politicians to try to work out some sort of a reasonable solution but with no success. The final decision by the Iraqi leadership: The treaty must go. Jabr rushed back to Baghdad to try to explain his position, but the riots continued. Jabr and his government were forced out of office, and the treaty was abandoned. The door to political power swung open once more, and once more Nuri as-Said walked in. Under his leadership, a new government was formed, filled once again with the same group of older politicians who had repeatedly held office since independence.

A NEW GENERATION

But the times were changing. A newer generation was eager for power, and the continuing conflict with Great Britain was of limited interest to them. Instead, their focus was on the need for social reform, to address the differences between the "haves" and "have-nots" in Iraqi society.

They argued that the current system was not governing all the people fairly; in fact, only a handful of people were enjoying the wealth and power while the rest struggled to earn enough for daily existence. Passionate about their cause, and with the support of students and political leaders opposed to the government, this group rioted in 1952. Order was restored only when the army marched in to control its own people. For two months, the army ruled the country under martial law before the government was once more in the hands of the older leadership.

By 1953, King Faisal II was 18 years old and ready to take over the duties of ruling his kingdom. But his uncle was reluctant to give up all his political power. So, while various groups struggled to gain power politically, a similar struggle was going on within the royal family. Hopes for a new political system under the new king grew increasingly dim as it became clear that the regent had no intention of completely handing control over to his nephew.

The development of Iraq's oil fields meant that riches were pouring into the country. But in the increasingly dissatisfied eyes of Iraq's younger generation, the same older leaders were enjoying all the power and wealth while making decisions at the expense of their countrymen. Many of these angry young men were in the military. They formed a group, known as the Free Officers (signifying "free" from military rules and the duty to a political authority they considered corrupt), and began to meet in secret to plan the overthrow of the government.

Many of these young soldiers had been drafted from poor families, and they knew from personal experience the inequality of the government's distribution of resources. They had seen their own families struggle for daily food, and once they were brought into the army, they observed firsthand the fine lifestyle that politicians and some of the higher-ranking military officials were enjoying.

While rumors swirled that violence was brewing, the Free Officers still managed a surprise attack. On July 13, 1958, army troops were ordered to march to Jordan to reinforce the Jordanian army against threats from Israel. The troops set out, but late in the evening they changed direction and marched instead

Instead of heading toward Jordan to assist their troops against Israel, the Iraqi army defied orders and turned around to march into Baghdad. After hearing about the revolution on the radio, Iraqis stormed the streets of Baghdad, excited and hopeful for a change in government.

to Baghdad, where they seized control of the city. Colonel Abd al-Salam'Arif led a team to the radio station, where at 5:00 A.M. on July 14, he began broadcasting messages to the public, stating that the revolution was underway and that they should rush to the streets to offer their support. At about the same time, another group of soldiers entered the royal palace. King Faisal

II, his uncle, and other members of the royal family rushed out to the front courtyard, no doubt intending to surrender, but they were immediately shot and killed.

With the king and regent dead, just one more link to the old regime was left: Nuri as-Said. The revolutionaries felt that, in order to successfully and symbolically signal the start of a new political era, not only the royal family but also as-Said must go.

Thus, early in the morning of July 14, as soldiers were attacking the palace and assassinating the royal family, a small group of soldiers surrounded as-Said's house. Awakened by the noise (and still wearing his pajamas), as-Said slipped out the back door and escaped. The streets were crowded with people awakened by the radio broadcasts and chattering excitedly about the revolution underway. Disguised as a woman, as-Said moved quickly from the house of one friend to another as soldiers began to search the area for him. A servant in one of the houses where he was hiding spotted him and raced for the door. Sensing that he was going to be betrayed, as-Said also raced out into the crowded streets. A young man noticed the "woman" walking nearby whose face and head was covered with a black gown but whose pajamas were peeking out underneath. He called out, "That is Nuri as-Said!" Knowing full well the fate that awaited him as soldiers turned toward him, Nuri as-Said pulled out his gun and killed himself.

The radio broadcasts that sounded throughout Baghdad on that July morning spoke of freedom, of new power for all Iraqis, and of a government inspired by and working for its people. Iraq would become a republic, with a president and officials elected by the people. The men who had earlier taken Iraq into a new era, who had brought about independence, seen it through two world wars, and shaped the fate of so many, had been erased in a hail of bullets.

6

A Country in Confusion

*T*he men who came to power in the aftermath of the 1958 revolution shared an overwhelming desire to bring about positive change, as well as a background in the military, although they differed on whether they were primarily Iraqi or Arab nationalists. Military forces had been in power once before, and then, as now, they were reluctant to hand over the government to civilian representatives.

They did take immediate steps to declare Iraq a republic whose official religion would be Islam. To emphasize ties with other Arab states, they declared that Iraq was an "integral part of the Arab nation." And rather than appointing a single person as the head of the new government, they set up a Sovereignty Council, consisting of three representatives who would be responsible for ruling the nation. But this was only a pretense: The real power and authority remained firmly in the hands of the military.

In fact, a power struggle was underway between two men who had been very involved in the revolution and who now wanted to be key players in the new government. Brigadier Abd al-Karim Qasim had led the Free Officers' movement and, as a senior military official, had quickly assumed a leading position in the new government. But Colonel Arif had headed up the march on Baghdad and had made the broadcasts announcing the revolution from the captured radio station. His voice and personality were identified by many as an important part of the launch of the new government, and he, too, sought to be a leader of the new government.

The differences between these two military leaders quickly became clear. Abd al-Karim Qasim came from an Arab family whose members included both Sunnis and Shiites. As a student, Qasim was remembered mainly for sitting in the back of his classes and for the evidence of his family's poverty in the shabby clothes he wore. After an unsuccessful but brief period as a teacher, Qasim decided to join the military. It was there that he found his calling, in an environment where social class mattered less than courage and hard work. The pride in one's own country that was an important part of military training greatly impressed Qasim. It is thus not surprising that once Qasim came to power the issues that mattered most to him included improving social conditions for the poor and emphasizing Iraq's own strength and status as an independent nation.

As head of the initial governing force, Qasim named himself head of the country's military and defense. He named Colonel Abd al-Salam' Arif his deputy commander. But Arif had a very different goal in mind for Iraq. He supported the idea of a "brotherhood of Arab nations," with all Arab countries joining together as part of a single nation, and he had assumed that his fellow military officers shared this dream. But he was wrong. A mere five days after the revolution, Arif and Qasim began to challenge each other, each taking up opposite positions on the issue of greatest importance: Would Iraq be an independent nation or would it become part of the United Arab Republic (UAR)?

The two men had been friends for many years, had served together in the military, and had planned the revolution with many of the same ideals in mind. They complemented each other in style and personality—Qasim was older, more serious and quiet, while Arif was bold, outspoken, and charming. But in the ruthless world of revolutionary politics, a friend can quickly be transformed into a foe. Qasim, as the senior officer, had no intention of allowing his friend to turn Iraq away from

As one of the two men who orchestrated the coup d'etat, Colonel Abd al-Salam´ Arif *(waving)* was popular among the Iraqi people, and his speeches were well received. Arif's vision of a united Arab state differed from that of Brigadier Abd al-Karim Qasim, who wanted an independent Iraq.

the destiny he thought best, and he began to quietly take steps to move his friend aside.

First, he sent Arif out on tours around the country, claiming that his appearances would serve to calm down the nervous citizens and explain the revolution's plans for the future. While Arif was away, Qasim replaced pro-Arab officers with pro-Communist men who supported maintaining Iraq as an independent nation. When Arif's speeches began to receive popular attention and support, Qasim began making his own speeches, some broadcast on radio and television. By November 1958, Qasim took another step to ensure his popularity by announcing salary increases for all government workers (which included a large percentage of the population).

Finally, Qasim removed Arif from the country altogether and from any significant position of influence: He appointed him ambassador to the German Federal Republic. Arif decided to resign instead and remained in the country, where a steady stream of officers who favored Arab unity began to meet and plan a revolution against the new revolutionary government. A series of meetings between Qasim and Arif failed to resolve their differences, and Arif was ultimately arrested and sentenced to death. But Qasim was unwilling to sign the paper authorizing the death of his former friend. So Arif was held in prison, with death sentences threatening him and his followers, for three long years.

POWER TO THE PARTY

Before the revolution, the few political parties that had had any significant influence were generally moderate and supported the people in power, mainly large landowners. But in order to be successful, the revolution had to persuade the Iraqi people not to accept business as usual, with the same political leaders making decisions. As it turned out, the people were easily convinced, but problems arose when the military leaders became the established political power. The changes they were able to bring about in the lives of the Iraqi people were generally small and insignificant. The desire for greater reform that they had sparked in the people with their revolutionary talk continued, and the people hungered for a political system that could make their lives noticeably better.

Two political parties stepped in to quietly urge the people on: the Communist Party and the Ba'ath (Arab Socialist) Party. Like Qasim and Arif, these two parties split over the issue of

Arab unity, with the Communists strongly favoring an independent nation of Iraq and the Ba'ath Party supporting the creation of a single Arab nation based on Socialist principles. Not surprisingly, each party backed the leader they felt best voiced their views.

Qasim did not allow this infighting to distract him from his goal of a strong Iraq. He knew that one path to greater stability lay in revenues from oil production. By 1961, he was meeting with representatives from the Iraq Petroleum Company to increase the share of Iraq's profits from oil production. The negotiations failed, so Qasim explored another route to increasing Iraq's oil profits: He decided to claim that the tiny emirate of Kuwait belonged to Iraq.

While there was some basis to the idea of a shared ethnic and historical background between the two countries dating back to the Ottoman Empire, Iraq's claim was scarcely likely to succeed, because other Arab countries, especially Egypt and Saudi Arabia, would oppose it. So why did Qasim decide to announce this move to acquire Kuwaiti territory?

The answer is simple and one that will be repeated in the subsequent troubled history of Iraq, as well as in the political events in many nations. By announcing his claim to Kuwait, Qasim was attempting to shift attention away from battles within his own country and to rally both sides with calls that would appeal to Iraqi national pride (the Communists) and a greater Arab community (the Ba'athists—supporters of the Ba'ath Party).

And it also helped that Kuwait had oil—lots of it. Kuwait's agreement with the oil companies operating within its borders gave it an even split in all profits from the oil, making Kuwait a very rich territory.

Upon hearing of Qasim's threats and rumors of troops gathering on the border, both the Arab League and Great Britain (which until earlier that year had occupied the territory of Kuwait) sent their own military forces in to protect the new state. Qasim never carried out his threats of force, but he suffered the consequences. Kuwait's independence was recognized by the other

Arab nations, and Qasim promptly severed diplomatic relations with these countries. When the crisis ended, Qasim found himself isolated from neighboring nations and facing an even more unsettled political future.

It was only a matter of time before the forces in Iraq opposing Qasim mobilized. An earlier attempt on Qasim's life (in 1959) had been unsuccessful, and the result was even stricter government controls on all aspects of daily life in an effort to stamp out rebellion. But the Ba'ath party took advantage of this government crackdown to lure supporters from among the increasingly dissatisfied Iraqi citizens.

A strike by high-school students provided the spark that launched another revolution. It began simply enough, with a fight between two high-school students. One of the students was the son of a high-ranking military official, who quickly intervened to protect his son from punishment. On December 27, 1962, students at the high school went on strike to protest this unfair favoritism, and they were joined by students from other high schools and from the University of Baghdad. The Ba'ath Party quickly moved in, capitalizing on the confusion and uproar to amplify the protests and unify certain parts of the military behind them. In February 1963, an attack was launched by Ba'ath supporters on certain regions around Baghdad. In a tactic familiar to veterans of the earlier revolution, early fighting focused on capturing the main radio station. Once Ba'ath supporters succeeded in this, broadcasts were quickly issued to the nation announcing the launch of a new government. The new president of this new government: Abd al-Salam' Arif.

The Communists did not accept this new government, believing that the American Central Intelligence Agency (CIA) was backing the Ba'ath Party and, instead, urged the public to rush to police stations, grab weapons, and attack the revolutionaries. Fierce fighting took place in the streets, until finally Qasim was persuaded to resign. He was taken to meet with Arif and asked Arif to let him leave the country. But Qasim would not enjoy an easy escape. A court-martial was called for the very day

Qasim surrendered, and he and several of his supporters were sentenced to death. During their trial, Qasim spoke proudly of all that he had accomplished and of the important role he had played in the shaping of Iraq following the revolution. But the court was unimpressed. Qasim was led into a small room, where he was shot.

A SHORT-LIVED RULE

The first step for the new Ba'athist government was to purge the military ranks of those remaining officers who had supported Qasim and opposed the goal of Arab unity. A series of extensive forced retirements brought a new group of military leaders to power, with Arif as their leader. Similar sweeps occurred in government offices and even schools and universities, where teachers who had favored Communism were arrested and imprisoned. While this ensured that the philosophy of the new government would be clearly voiced by all in positions of authority, it also meant that the government, military, and educational systems would be run by largely inexperienced people, some lacking any credentials other than their support of the new government.

The new regime had three main aims: reestablishing military rule (with Arif at the head as president); reinforcing the importance of Arab unity; and emphasizing the ideals of Socialism, involving the nationalization of several large companies and banks. This last step was quite unpopular, and, as a result, Arif began to distance himself both from Socialism and from the military officers who put him in power. By 1965, a new government was formed (with Arif's support) with Abd ar-Rahman al-Bazzaz serving as premier.

Although he was a strong supporter of Arab unity, al-Bazzaz was no fan of military officials meddling in politics. Shortly after becoming premier, al-Bazzaz called for general elections and the establishment of a representative system of government. He also took steps to support private business interests within Iraq, working to create a balance between nationalized industries and the privately held businesses that played an important role in Iraq's economy. Arif decided to go on a speaking tour to raise public support for these new steps and to confirm his approval of al-Bazzaz's actions. In early April 1966, Arif set out on a tour of the southern provinces. His speeches were well received, but Arif's political triumph was to be short-lived. Returning from one of these speeches the evening of April 13, Arif's helicopter crashed shortly after takeoff. All aboard were killed.

The country genuinely mourned the death of Arif, and it may be due to this sentimental outpouring of grief that,

After the death of Colonel Arif, the Ba'ath Party staged another uprising and sent Arif's brother, who was serving as president, into exile. The Ba'ath party then chose Ahmad Hassan al-Bakr *(right)* as the new Iraqi president. Assisting al-Bakr with the reorganization of the Ba'ath Party was his aide and rising politician, Saddam Hussein *(left)*.

in the elections that followed, Arif's older brother, Abd ar-Rahman'Arif, was elected the new president. He quickly bowed to military pressure to remove al-Bazzaz from power, and by August 1966 the cabinet had resigned. A subsequent series of bad decisions—poor handling of Kurdish uprisings in the north, widespread corruption among those in power, the decision not to support other Arab states during the Arab-Israeli War of 1967—led to great unrest and dissatisfaction among the Iraqis. To make matters worse, the government never followed through on the promise al-Bazzaz had made to call for national elections.

The government depended solely on the military to retain power. The weakness of this situation became particularly evident in 1968, when a few key military officers who had been lured away by representatives of the Ba'ath Party led an attack on the president's palace.

In the predawn hours of July 17, the phone next to the president's bed rang. When he answered it, he was told by General Hardan al-Tikriti, a Ba'ath officer, "You are no longer president. The Ba'ath has taken control of your country. If you surrender peacefully, I can guarantee that your safety will be ensured." In attempting to determine if the call was a hoax, the president learned that the army had turned against him. Well aware of the bloody end to previous governments, he slowly walked to the palace entrance and surrendered. Only a few hours after receiving that fateful phone call, Arif was on a plane for London.

The new Ba'ath regime established a new political force, the Revolutionary Command Council, and selected a new president, Ahmad Hassan al-Bakr. This leader was responsible for the reorganization of the Ba'ath Party and for ensuring the party's new success. One of his assistants was a ruthless young man who had attempted to assassinate Qasim many years earlier and who more recently had spent time in prison for trying to overthrow the government. He joined al-Bakr in leading Iraq into a new era of Ba'ath leadership. His name was Saddam Hussein.

The Politics
of Power

The recent history of Iraq is closely identified with the personality and actions of Saddam Hussein, and so it is important to study the many twists and turns that led him to the presidency. In many ways, the events that shaped Saddam Hussein as a young man would, in turn, cause him to shape the destiny of his native land.

Saddam was born on April 28, 1937, in Tikrit, a small town about 100 miles north of Baghdad. As discussed earlier in this book, the late 1930s were a time of great political confusion in Iraq, with frequently changing governments and World War II looming on the horizon. But the town of Tikrit was far removed from the hectic swirl of political maneuvering and forces of change. Saddam's family, like the majority of people in the area, lived in a mud hut and burned cow dung for fuel. They had no electricity or running water. There was only one paved road in the entire town. Saddam's father abandoned his wife and died before Saddam was born, and his mother, unable to take care of the infant, left him to be raised by his uncle Khairallah.

The name Saddam means "one who confronts," and Saddam's childhood, marked by sadness and violence, gave him plenty of reasons to live up to his name. His uncle, a military man, had participated in the thwarted Iraqi uprising of April 1941 against British troops at the air base at Habbaniya. When the monarchy was restored and the British regained power, those who had participated in the violence were jailed (and some even executed).

Saddam's uncle was imprisoned for five years. In later years, Saddam's sympathy for his uncle's experience would become clear in his own distrust of foreign meddling in Iraqi politics and a definite disgust with the monarchy.

After his uncle was jailed, Saddam was sent back to live with his mother. By then she had remarried, and his stepfather treated him with cruelty. He was forced to steal, was subjected to frequent beatings, and lived a miserable, lonely life until his uncle was released from prison in 1947. Saddam was permitted to return to his uncle's home in Tikrit where, for the first time, at the age of 10, he was allowed to go to school. Studies were a struggle, particularly since Saddam was behind most of his fellow students, and he spent more time on practical jokes than on learning. In one particularly nasty prank, Saddam approached his teacher with open arms, gave him an apparently friendly hug, and then quickly slipped a snake under his robe.

His poor grades kept him from enrolling in the military academy—a terrible disappointment to the young man who had dreamed of a career in the military. In fact, this dream was never forgotten. It would finally be fulfilled some 20 years later when Saddam would receive the honorary rank of general despite never having served in the military.

When Saddam was rejected by the military academy, he moved with his uncle to Baghdad in 1955 to enroll in high school. Baghdad was quite a different environment from the mud huts and dirt roads of his birthplace. The town was buzzing with political plots and tales of spies. Intrigue was everywhere, and Saddam quickly was caught up in the widespread public complaints and riots that were turning Baghdad into a dangerously unstable city. The sense of dissatisfaction, the undercurrent of violence, and the plotting all were perfectly suited to Saddam's personality, and he joined the Ba'ath Party at the age of 20, strongly believing in its message of Arab unity and its antigovernment activities.

When Saddam first became a member, the Ba'ath Party was quite small, with only about 300 members. There were many political parties in Iraq at the time, and it is interesting that

Saddam chose to join one of the less powerful ones in operation. However, the motto of the party, "One Arab Nation with an Eternal Mission," made clear its goal: the unification of all Arab peoples and countries into a single, powerful national force—a goal for which his uncle had fought many years ago against the British and for which, ultimately, he had been put in prison.

Also known as the Arab Socialist Party, the Ba'ath Party swept up many young men like Saddam in its activities. The Ba'ath Party was particularly appealing to younger Iraqi political activists because its goal of a unified Arab nation was accompanied by economic plans that were designed to modernize Iraqi society. It was, in a way, a political party that was rebelling against the ideas of an older generation of Iraqi politicians, seeking new and revolutionary ways to make life in Iraq better.

Saddam Hussein's earliest political actions involved persuading his classmates to participate in activities designed to destabilize the government. He formed a kind of political gang that roamed the streets frightening citizens and attacking political opponents. At the age of 21, he was imprisoned briefly in connection with the murder of a government official, although there was ultimately not enough evidence to connect him to the crime. But the experience brought him to the attention of party officials and his next assignment was a dramatic one—to assassinate Abd al-Karim Qasim, the leader of Iraq.

FROM PARTY MAN TO WANTED MAN

While driving home from his office on the night of October 7, 1959, Qasim was attacked in his car by Saddam and several other young party members. The nation's leader was wounded in the hail of bullets, but he managed to escape. Saddam's role in the assassination attempt was later embellished by Saddam and his admirers. Apparently, his actual assignment was to provide covering fire for the other attackers, who were to kill Qasim. But according to most reports, he instead opened fire himself on Qasim, no doubt confusing the rest of his fellow attackers and giving the leader's bodyguards a chance to fight back. Saddam was shot—by one of the members of his own team—and the legend of his escape includes an amazing tale of flight, first on horseback, then by swimming across the freezing Tigris River with a knife clutched between his teeth. Later, he would use the knife to remove the bullet from his own body when he was unable to get medical help.

Whether or not every element of this story is true, it is clear that the assassination attempt made him famous in the Ba'ath Party and ensured him a warm welcome by party members living in Syria once he fled across the border. From Syria, Saddam went on to Egypt, where he became involved in political activity and, at the same time, finally graduated from high school at the age of 24.

Saddam decided to enroll in law school in Cairo but did not complete his studies. He eventually received a law degree, although not due to any exceptional academic effort. Nine years after dropping out of law school in Egypt, he appeared at the University of Baghdad with a pistol in his belt, surrounded by four bodyguards. The law degree was quickly produced.

During his three-year stay in Egypt, Saddam also selected his wife. His fiancée was his cousin, Sajidah Talfah, who had grown up with him in his uncle Khairallah's home. They were married when Saddam moved back to Iraq in 1963. The reason for his return: The Ba'ath Party had seized power.

A PARTY IN CHAOS

On his return to Iraq, Saddam Hussein found that the Ba'ath Party, and his role in it, had greatly changed. While the assassination attempt on Qasim had made Saddam somewhat famous in the party at the time, three years had passed and a different group of leaders was now directing the party's activities. Rushing home with the idea that he would be involved in shaping the destiny of his country, Saddam discovered instead that he had essentially been forgotten during his absence.

The ambitious young man soon realized that political power comes not merely from daring actions but also from networking. In the quickly shifting Iraqi political environment at the time, it was critical to have as many friends in high places as possible, and Saddam soon set to work making himself useful to many powerful people in the Ba'ath Party.

From the moment they assumed power, the Ba'athists demonstrated a preference for brute force over polite debate. They

Saddam Hussein returned to Baghdad when the Ba'athists took power in 1963. Their use of force and intimidation was known throughout the country, and they sent the military *(above)* to round up dissidents, like suspected Communists, to eliminate opposition.

were absolutely ruthless in their treatment of political opponents, and their methods were designed not only to demonstrate their political power but also to intimidate anyone thinking of working against them. For example, during their first days in charge of the government, following the actual assassination of Qasim, the Ba'athists learned that rumors were circulating among the people that Qasim was not really dead, that perhaps he was in hiding somewhere and would soon return to overthrow the Ba'ath regime. It did not take the new government long to decide how to put an end to that rumor. For several nights, Iraqis fortunate enough to own a television would turn it on to be greeted by the sight of Qasim's bloody body and the battered corpses of his fellow officials. The camera even showed close-ups of each of the bullet holes in Qasim's body.

The violence was not reserved just for the former rulers but extended also to anyone who threatened the Ba'ath's power. The stately palace from which King Faisal and his family had ruled over Iraq only a short time earlier was transformed into Qasr-al-Nihayyah, the "Palace of the End." The place where the king had been shot to death in 1958 became the place where many political prisoners would meet even more grisly fates during the Ba'ath Party's time in power. It is believed by many that one of Saddam's jobs in the new government was to serve as an interrogator, and when the Ba'ath Party was finally overthrown by the American invasion in 2003, the horrifying evidence of torture at the palace was revealed, including electric wires with pincers, pointed iron stakes on which prisoners were forced to sit, and a machine used to chop off fingers.

While the party reacted swiftly and brutally to any political opposition, it soon became clear that the greatest threat to the Ba'athists was to be found within their own ranks. Almost as soon as it came to power, the Ba'ath Party began to break apart—a victim of differing viewpoints. Some in the party felt that the changes needed to transform Iraq into the ideal Arab

Socialist nation should happen quickly, using force if necessary. A different group supported working with those outside the party to achieve change more slowly. A third group tried to bridge the gap, favoring more practical approaches while at the same time pushing for Socialist goals. In this group was Iraq's president, Ahmad Hassan Al-Bakr, and it was with him that Saddam was to establish an important link.

Meanwhile, the internal fighting among Ba'ath members ultimately meant disaster. Unable to achieve any kind of unity, it was impossible to make decisions, and the party and the country descended into chaos. The more radical representatives of the party were arrested and forced out of the country, and riots quickly broke out in Baghdad. After a brief nine months in power, the Ba'aths lost control of the government, and the key party members were forced out of the country, killed, or thrown in prison.

Saddam decided to remain in Iraq, and he was soon put in jail. For two years he used his prison sentence as an opportunity to network with other political prisoners and to educate himself in political strategy by reading and debating with other imprisoned members of the party. He kept in contact with Bakr by smuggling out messages in the clothes of his infant child when his wife and baby would visit him.

Ultimately, Saddam devised an escape plan involving two of his fellow prisoners who were scheduled to appear in court with him on a certain day. As they traveled to their trial, the three prisoners pleaded with their guards to stop at a particular restaurant in Baghdad for lunch. When they agreed, Saddam and one of the other prisoners went to the bathroom and escaped out the window to a waiting getaway car.

Saddam Hussein had learned several important lessons during the Ba'ath Party's first experience heading the government. He made sure that when the next opportunity came, he would be ready—and that this time he would be playing a much bigger role.

MIGHT MAKES RIGHT

Saddam's smuggled messages to Bakr did their work. As one of the few more senior Ba'ath Party members still in Iraq, Bakr became a powerful force within the party as it struggled to rebuild. And Saddam was by his side, serving as assistant and right-hand man, and eventually he was appointed to a key position in the party's Revolutionary Command Council, the organization responsible for directing party activities.

Saddam recognized that, in the shifting sands of Iraqi politics, one single element ensured power: physical force. The recent history of quickly changing governments proved that power was achieved not through garnering popular support or making wise political deals (although these were helpful), but rather by seizing it with force. That was why the military had so often taken over governments—they possessed in numbers and weapons the greatest force, and they did not hesitate to use them. Without their own military wing, the Ba'aths had been unable to fight off the takeover of their own government. Saddam recognized that, in order to fight their way back into power, the Ba'aths would have to be willing to demonstrate, and ultimately use, sheer force.

And so they did, when then-president Abd al-Rahman Arif woke up on the morning of July 17, 1968, to learn that he was no longer the leader of Iraq. Saddam was not a critical player in the early days of the "July Revolution," as it became known. Instead, he was working behind the scenes as his mentor, Bakr, joined a team of other Ba'ath officials in shaping the new government. Bakr became president, but a number of other officials continued to vie for power, and the arguments and internal fighting that had doomed the Ba'ath Party the first time it seized power occurred again. But Saddam had learned his lesson well, and he quickly moved to stamp out any rivals to Bakr. One rival, the minister of defense, Ibrahim Da'ud, was sent out of the country on a mission to inspect the Iraqi troops stationed in Jordan and then not allowed to return. The other, Premier Abd al Razzaq Nayif, was forced to leave the country by a gun-toting Saddam and his officers after he had been

As the second most powerful man in Iraq after the July Revolution, Saddam Hussein *(center, facing crowd)* chose to raise his public profile through intimidation. In 1969, he personally inspected the gallows where 14 so-called "spies of Israel" were hanged in Liberation Square in Baghdad. He later addressed the crowd who had gathered to witness the executions *(above)*.

invited to a luncheon with President Bakr. Nayif was escorted to a waiting car and then to a plane headed for Morocco.

Within two weeks, the second phase of the July Revolution was completed, and power was firmly in the hands of Bakr and his choice for deputy chairman: Saddam Hussein. At the age of 31, Saddam had become the second most powerful man in Iraq.

Saddam personally chose to head up the security services of the Ba'ath Party, and in this capacity, one of his first acts was to wipe out any traces of opposition. Horrifying stories exist of the brutal ways in which non-Ba'athists were removed from all government offices, including the military. Key military officers were retired and, in many cases, arrested and tortured. Their positions were all filled by men loyal only to Saddam.

For the next few years, Saddam kept a low public profile, all the time working behind the scenes to remove opponents and cement the power of the Ba'ath Party. In the early days of the July Revolution, while the party was at its weakest, Saddam was at his most invisible, wisely deciding that should the government be overthrown yet again, he would be at the head of the list of those who would be removed from office. He was a loyal assistant to Bakr, and he refused to make the mistake many of his predecessors had made—seizing job titles and privileges as a right. Instead, he constantly sought ways to make the party stronger and its position at the head of the government more certain. The Ba'ath Party, which had not been terribly popular at the time of the July Revolution, gradually gained members as it became clear that important government and military jobs would be granted only to party members.

By 1973, the military and security forces no longer posed a threat to the government; they were filled with Ba'ath members, all loyal to the party but particularly loyal to Saddam. Political opponents had either been killed or fled Iraq. Periodically, a trial of some real or imagined group of political activists would be broadcast and the resulting executions would clearly demonstrate to the Iraqi people that an unpleasant fate awaited those who dreamed of a new system of government.

PROGRESS AND THE PRESIDENCY

Saddam Hussein used not only threats but also economic development to ensure popular support for the government. While he was still officially in the number two position in the government, it was becoming clear that more and more of the decisions were being made by Saddam. Feeling more confident of the party's success, he was willing to step into the spotlight.

Both Saddam and the Ba'ath Party benefited from the nationalization of Iraq's oil industry and the wealth that came from that oil. Some of the money was distributed to Iraqis in the form of tax cuts and pay increases; other benefits included free education from kindergarten through college. In fact, many of Saddam's programs were quite progressive, both for Iraq and for the Arab world. He led several campaigns to stamp out illiteracy, and he also supported legislation guaranteeing equal pay and equal job opportunities for women (including laws passed to permit women to join the military). It was clear, however, that Saddam was moving away from trying to unite the Arabs and focusing instead on keeping stability and power within his own country's borders.

The winds of change were blowing in the Persian Gulf, and Saddam was mindful that power, no matter how long held, could vanish in a puff of revolutionary smoke. By 1978, the Shah of Iran (whose family had ruled since 1925) was struggling to keep his country from descending into chaos. Riots and public demonstrations made it clear that Iraq's eastern neighbor was facing the prospect of civil war. Many felt that the riots were being incited by Ayatollah Khomeini, an Iranian religious leader who had been forced out of his own country and had been living in Iraq since 1964. At the request of the Shah, Saddam Hussein forced the Ayatollah to leave Iraq for France, but the unrest in Iran intensified. The Shah was overthrown and the Ayatollah returned to rule Iran, preaching an Islamist message that included a plan to spread the religious fever that had sparked Iran's revolution to other nations.

This was not a happy message for Saddam. He decided that the rumblings on the other side of the eastern border needed a strong response, and he knew that he was the one to give it. The

Leaving behind the idea of Arab unity and independence throughout the region, Saddam Hussein instead turned his attention to maintaining power in Iraq. When the Shah of Iran asked for Ayatollah Khomeini *(above, left)*, an Iranian cleric and critic of the monarchy, to be removed from his exile in Iraq, Hussein quickly responded and ejected Khomeini. The religious figure of the Iranian revolution eventually returned to Iran to cause political turmoil with Hussein later.

time had come for him to become, firmly and decisively, the undisputed leader of Iraq.

He set out on a whirlwind tour of Iraq, making speeches and visiting different locations—military bases, Ba'ath Party offices, big cities, and small towns—accompanied by the news media. Now he was ready for the spotlight, and at every opportunity he stepped into it. His speeches were printed word for word in newspapers, and his picture was everywhere. He was never outwardly disloyal to his boss, President Bakr, but the message was clear: He was the new leader in Iraq.

On July 16, 1979, nearly 11 years to the day after the Ba'ath Party had taken over Iraq, President Bakr appeared on television and announced that he was ready to retire. The change in leadership was swift. Immediately after Bakr's announcement, Saddam Hussein was sworn in as the president of Iraq.

A BLOODY BEGINNING

On July 22, six days after becoming president, Saddam called a meeting of the top 1,000 members of the Ba'ath Party. Those invited no doubt expected to listen to their new leader's plans for the future, perhaps with promises for increased prestige for party members or even details of new economic goals or successes. Instead, they heard something quite different.

The meeting began with a high-level official reading a confession, in which he admitted participating in a conspiracy against the government, supposedly with the support of Syria. Saddam immediately responded, denouncing traitors and those disloyal to the party. He then announced, "The people whose names I am going to read out should repeat the slogan of the party and leave the hall." Slowly he read out a list of more than 60 names, many of them the leading men in Iraq. One by one, they were taken from the room and executed. Others would soon follow. In the days after that meeting, many members of the Ba'ath Party followed Saddam's directions to seek out "traitors" among their former friends and colleagues. Some estimates indicate that nearly 500 men were killed during those first few days of Saddam Hussein's presidency. It is clear that he effectively eliminated any possible rivals, sparked fear among those who might have been dreaming of competing with him for power, and began a system of friend reporting on friend and neighbor spying on neighbor that would transform Iraq into a police state in which no one was ever completely safe.

8

The Road to War

At the age of 42, Saddam Hussein was a mighty force within Iraq, simultaneously serving as president, secretary-general of the Ba'ath party, commander in chief, head of the government, and chairman of the Revolutionary Command Council. His presence was felt everywhere, staring down at the Iraqi people from posters, announcing decrees in newspapers and on the television and radio, even beaming up at them from the faces of gold watches. He took to popping in unexpectedly at hospitals and factories, showing the Iraqi people not only that he cared about them, but also that he could be anywhere and everywhere.

Saddam understood the importance of television and exploited it to demonstrate his connection with the Iraqi people. One of his favorite venues was a regularly televised program in which he, in disguise, would drop in on an ordinary Iraqi family. The family would pretend not to recognize their president. Saddam would ask them for their opinion of the government, and the family would spend several minutes praising their president and his policies. Then Saddam would take off his disguise and the family would express first their amazement and then their joy that their beloved leader was in their humble home.

But the lighter moments in Saddam's presidency were becoming rare as he increasingly concentrated on confronting pressures from his neighbor to the east. The new governing powers in Iran were hoping to export their revolution across the border—to overthrow Saddam's government (which the strictly religious Ayatollah viewed as not nearly devout enough) and

Saddam Hussein carried many names during his reign: the Anointed One, Glorious Leader, Direct Descendent of the Prophet, Great Uncle, and President of Iraq. His propaganda machine churned out embellished newspaper stories, and Iraqis constantly felt his presence due to the large murals and giant statues that were present everywhere.

replace it with the kind of conservative Shiite regime operating in Iran. This was not an idle threat. In Iraq, a Sunni minority held power over the rest of the nation. Approximately 60 percent of Iraqis were Shiite, and they were becoming increasingly unhappy with the Ba'ath party.

In June 1979, the Ayatollah's regime in Iran began broadcasting messages that urged the Iraqi population to overthrow Saddam's government. Over the next several months, at least 20 Iraqi officials were killed in bomb attacks attributed to Shiite activists. In April 1980, the Iraqi deputy prime minister, Tariq Aziz, was nearly killed while giving a speech at a university in Baghdad.

The tension continued over the next several months until September 4, when Iranian forces shelled some of the towns along the Iraqi border. Saddam had had enough. On September 22, 1980, Iraq launched an attack against Iranian air bases. Iran retaliated by bombing Iraqi military and economic targets, while Iraqi armed forces crossed the border and launched additional land-based attacks, focusing on Iran's oil fields and refineries.

Iraq benefited from the element of surprise in its initial attack, but Saddam's motives were defensive rather than offensive, and this caused him to make a costly mistake. Rather than taking advantage of his army's initial gains and successes, he halted its advance and then tried to negotiate a cease-fire agreement. The Iraqi army, pumped up from its early success, was frustrated at seeing its efforts halted and at being denied the opportunity to press ahead and gain additional territory. While Saddam tried to negotiate a cease-fire, the Iranian forces used the time to reorganize their troops. Saddam's attempts to end the war failed, and his troops soon found themselves bogged down in a life-and-death struggle with Iran's forces. Saddam's plan for a quick and decisive fight had failed. His army and his country would pay the price.

WAR IN THE GULF

By November 1980, Iraq's initial successes had faded. The Iranian army had been able to regroup and successfully maintained their position, and for the next 10 months the two armies fought fiercely, neither side gaining or losing any significant amount of land. But the number of casualties were beginning to pile up at an alarming rate.

The two countries took very different approaches to the war. In Iran, the Ayatollah urged his people to make sacrifices and to dedicate their precious resources to the war cause, because it was a holy war whose aim was pure and good. In Iraq, Saddam Hussein instead assumed a business as usual attitude, and, initially, most Iraqi people did not feel the effects of the war. Food and goods were still generally available. The only significant difference noticed in the capital was that more women were taking the jobs that previously had been held by men, more and more of whom were serving in the armed forces.

The cost of maintaining the army while shielding the Iraqi people from any kind of significant shortages was enormous. Saddam soon made it clear to his neighbors to the south and west, Kuwait and Saudi Arabia, that the war Iraq was fighting was not some minor border dispute. Indeed, the Ayatollah in Iran had made clear that his goal was to ensure the spread of Shiite Muslim leadership throughout the entire Gulf region. Saddam made sure that the other Gulf countries were well aware of this goal, and that Iraq's role as a buffer, shielding its neighbors from the spread of Iranian revolution, would not be able to continue without their financial support.

For many Arab leaders, the choice was clear. The Ayatollah's stated goal of "exporting the revolution" threatened all of them. They felt that the spread of Iran's Islamic revolution would mean the end of any plans for Arab unity. The aims of Arabic nationalism were generally progressive, while the Iranian movement, based on conservative religious goals, planned a very different destiny for the Gulf states, one which deprived these leaders of their power. But Iraq's neighbors were hesitant about committing themselves to either side, perhaps fearing the consequences to their cities and oil fields of joining the war, or perhaps not completely certain which side posed the greater threat if it should win the war. But support for the Iraqi side eventually came. First Jordan, then Saudi Arabia, and finally Egypt sided with Iraq. Syria and Libya offered their support to the Iranians.

The alliances came about as the war took a new and dangerous twist. The Iraqi army, increasingly embattled and growing tired as it struggled to maintain its positions in Iranian territory, was becoming less and less willing to fight. Wisely sensing this change in his soldiers' morale, Saddam announced that he would pull his soldiers out of Iranian territory, claiming that they were needed to help the Lebanese fight off invading Israeli troops. The troop withdrawals began on June 20, 1982.

This action, however, did not move the Iranians toward peace. In fact, it did the opposite. A mere 23 days after the Iraqis began their retreat, Iranian troops launched a massive attack on Iraqi soil, this time targeting the important port city of Basra, which is a relatively short distance from Kuwait and Saudi Arabia. This time, Saddam had little trouble persuading the leaders of these two countries to come to his assistance. Both pledged billions of dollars in support for the Iraqi war cause, providing Saddam much-needed funds at a time when the Iraqi people were beginning to feel the effects of a war suddenly being fought inside their own borders. Aid also came from outside the Gulf, as countries such as the United States, the Soviet Union, and France provided Iraq with military supplies, intelligence reports, and food and other goods. Many of these supplies enabled Iraq to expand its production of chemical and biological weapons, which would be used, 10 years later, to threaten the very allies who had come to Saddam's aid.

The war raged on for a long and devastating eight years. Saddam frequently attempted to negotiate peace, at the end asking only for an agreement that each side respect the other's government (in other words, he was asking for peace with the simple request that the Iranians agree to call off their plans to overthrow his regime). Even this was ignored by the Iranians. But their unyielding posture would prove costly in the long run. Supplied with weapons and financial support from powerful allies, and fighting battles to defend his own soil, Saddam was able to rally the Iraqi people. The Iranian army, on the other hand, was exhausted from years of fighting on foreign land. Sensing the shift, Saddam ordered a sudden fierce attack. From February to April 1988, missiles and air attacks (some allegations suggest that poison gas was used) were launched against the largest cities in Iran. The people fled the cities in huge numbers, and the government was threatened as its support vanished.

It was the beginning of the end for the Iranian initiative. Lacking enough volunteers for its army, and with the citizens who had brought them to power turning against the leaders who had led them into the war, the Iranian government began to look for a way out. The Iraqi army continued its fierce campaigns, recapturing lost ground. By July 18, 1988, Iran agreed to accept the United Nations Security Council's resolution calling for a cease-fire that Iraq had accepted one year earlier. It took one more month for the message to be spread along all the military bases and then, finally, the fighting was over.

THE FINAL VICTIMS

Though the war with Iran had ended, Saddam had not completed his military campaign. Unfortunately, the most brutal phase of the war occurred after the cease-fire had been agreed to and the shelling on the borders had ended.

During the war, the Iranian government had taken advantage of the always unstable relationship between Iraq and its Kurdish population to incite additional fighting between them. The Kurds had been seeking their own state since the Middle East was divided following World War I—a state they had been promised but never received. Ever since, they had engaged in struggles for independence in Turkey, Iraq, and Iran. The Iranians had promised to assist the Iraqi Kurds in their efforts—and extended the possibility of a Kurdish region of their own—if they would fight with the Iranians against the Iraqis. Many Iraqi Kurds, feeling that they had been abused by their government, were willing to do so.

Living in an area that encompasses land from four Middle Eastern nations—
Turkey, Syria, Iran, and Iraq—the Kurds have their own distinct culture and language. Because of the oppression they experienced in Iraq, the Kurds supported
Iran during the Iran–Iraq War. Hussein retaliated against the Kurds in Iraq with
chemical weapons, with his most brutal and well-documented attack occuring in
the city of Halabja. Here, a girl from Halabja holds a picture of her family, victims
of the chemical weapons attack.

Saddam did not forget the Kurds' decision. Rather than seeking out only those who had participated in the fighting on behalf of Iran (many of whom had fled as the end of the war grew near), Saddam decided to eliminate the Kurdish "issue" altogether. Only five days after the cease-fire went into effect, Saddam launched a chemical weapon attack against 65 Kurdish villages. Iraqi war planes and helicopters flew over their northern territory, this time bringing death to the country's own people.

Many Kurds died instantly. According to reports from villagers, the weapons were not loud. As the bombs fell, first a weak sound was heard, and then a thin yellow mist spread out in a cloud from the area of impact. The air was filled with a foul smell, and then the villagers began to fall to the ground in a violent, choking death. One Kurdish survivor of the attack later reported: "In our village, 200 to 300 people died. All the animals and birds died. All the trees dried up. It smelled like something burned. The whole world turned yellow."

About 100,000 Kurdish refugees moved in terror toward Iraq's borders with Turkey and Iran. Those who were unable to escape were seized by Iraqi forces and divided into male and female groups. The women were sent to concentration camps; the men were executed.

When other countries learned of the brutal, murderous weapons Saddam had unleashed against his own people, the international community was outraged, although little concrete action was taken to help the Kurds. Saddam was surprised by the protests from those who had been allied with him just a short while earlier. After all, he was simply eliminating his enemies. Iraq was back to business as usual.

Storms in the Desert

In the aftermath of the war with Iran, Saddam Hussein found himself confronted with a crushing debt to those countries that had aided him. Allies like the United States and France, who had provided him with much-needed weapons and supplies, denounced his actions against the Kurds loudly in public, and yet in private chose to take no decisive action to back up their harsh words. Kuwait and Saudi Arabia were demanding repayment for loans made—a demand that angered Saddam, because he felt that Iraq had held back the Iranian revolutionary army, in a sense protecting its neighbors from having to defend themselves. When it became clear that Iraq would not repay its debt in the immediate future, Kuwait decided to deal with the cash shortage in another way: It increased its oil ouput. The Organization of Petroleum Exporting Countries (OPEC), to which Iraq, Kuwait, and other oil-producing nations belonged, had established limits on how much oil each country could produce, to ensure that the price stayed at an agreed upon cost per barrel. As Kuwait increased production, more oil became available to all buyers and the price per barrel began to drop. The loss in oil revenue was particularly damaging to Iraq, since, in the aftermath of the war, the income was desperately needed for the necessary rebuilding of war-devastated areas.

Saddam was in no mood to negotiate reasonably. He sent his foreign minister, Tariq Aziz, to a meeting of the Arab League in July 1990 to make Iraq's claims clear. Iraq demanded that Kuwait and the United Arab Emirates stop their overproduction of oil, that Kuwait forgive the Iraqi debt for loans made during

The international response to Iraq's invasion of Kuwait was to impose economic and aid sanctions against the Arab nation. Countries in the United Nations were forbidden to help Iraq, resulting in drastic food shortages and starvation. Critics claim over a million people—mostly children—died because of the imposed sanctions. These children are in line at a mosque food bank.

the war with Iran, and that the Gulf countries assist Iraq with its rebuilding efforts in war-torn areas.

The Kuwaitis, accustomed to Saddam's frequent bluster, perhaps naively chose to ignore these demands, assuming that he was simply trying to find a way to avoid repaying their loan. But the issue of disputed border areas should have raised red flags. The somewhat makeshift arrangements the British had made when granting Kuwait its independence in 1961 had left borders and territorial claims vague and in dispute.

Kuwait's fabulous oil wealth could provide Iraq with control of more than 20 percent of the world's oil production. And its location would give Iraq greater strategic access to the Gulf itself.

The next step came quickly. On August 2, 1990, an army of 100,000 Iraqi troops and 300 tanks rolled across the Kuwait–Iraq border. The Kuwaiti army, a mere 16,000 men, was no match for this invasion force. The Kuwait emir (the ruler of the tiny country) and his family fled their land, and the armed forces quickly surrendered.

On that very day, the United Nations Security Council passed a resolution demanding Iraq's immediate withdrawal from Kuwait. Saddam refused, and four days later the United Nations passed a second resolution, this one calling for economic sanctions against the aggressor. These sanctions meant that members of the UN were forbidden to sell or give weapons, food, or supplies to Iraq, nor were they allowed to purchase Iraqi oil.

The United States was among those nations speaking out most strongly against the Iraqi invasion of Kuwait. The administration of President George H.W. Bush viewed with alarm the movement of Iraqi troops heading toward Kuwait's border with Saudi Arabia. If the Saudis were similarly overrun by Iraqi troops, Saddam would control nearly 45 percent of the world's oil and pose an economic and military threat to all the nations in the Gulf region and to all oil-importing nations. By August 9, intense negotiations between the United States and Saudi Arabia led to an agreement to deploy American troops along the Saudi border.

During the next few tense months, several attempts at negotiations were made. To Saddam's surprise, many of his former allies joined the outcry against his seizure of Kuwait. The Iraqi people, still reeling from the effects of the war with Iran, now found themselves suffering the consequences of an economic blockade, making access to food and supplies increasingly difficult. The UN issued a statement declaring that force could be used against Iraq if it did not withdraw from Kuwaiti territory by January 15, 1991. And yet, Saddam refused to budge.

On January 9, 1991, the U.S. secretary of state, James Baker, met with the Iraqi foreign minister, Tariq Aziz, carrying a letter from then-U.S. president George H.W. Bush. The letter, intended for Saddam, clearly warned of the consequences of ignoring the order to withdraw from Kuwaiti soil and stated that Iraq stood at the brink of war with the rest of the world. Aziz refused to carry the letter to Saddam. A coalition of 28 nations now stood prepared to answer Iraqi actions in Kuwait with force.

MISSILES TARGET BAGHDAD

Shortly after midnight on January 17, 1991, allied planes began bombing Baghdad, shelling the capital and other strategic points throughout the country. Military bases and oil fields were the favored targets. The initial attack destroyed Saddam's presidential palace, the defense ministry, and the Ba'ath Party headquarters.

The devastating attacks were called "Operation Desert Storm" by the allied forces and "the Mother of All Battles" by Saddam Hussein. Despite the exaggerated descriptions and conflicting reports of victory by each side, it was clear that the Iraqis (particularly those living in Baghdad) were suffering greatly. As shelling continued, the country's major infrastructure was crumbling. Daily life was becoming increasingly miserable due to shortages of supplies, the absence of electricity or running water, and nightly rushes to air-raid shelters. The oil Saddam had seized meant little if it could not be sold and if, in fact, many of the Iraqi oil fields were being simultaneously destroyed by allied bombings.

As the cost of the war weighed heavier on the Iraqi people, Saddam made a surprising announcement: He indicated that he would withdraw Iraqi troops from Kuwait on condition that Israel began to withdraw from Palestine, the land it was currently occupying and which Saddam claimed was truly Arab

After devastating air strikes took their toll on the Iraqi government and its citizens, a coalition of forces launched a ground offensive to expel Hussein's forces from Kuwait. Many Iraqi soldiers surrendered when confronted by coalition forces (*above*), bringing a quick end to a tense conflict.

territory. The attempt to link Iraqi aggression with Israel's presence in the Middle East failed.

President Bush offered another deadline: Iraqi troops must withdraw from Kuwait by February 23, 1991, or a ground war would begin. When this deadline was not met, on February 24 the allied military forces quickly penetrated Iraqi defenses and, within two days, had taken control of Kuwait and were pushing north into Iraq. Early on the morning of February 28, as the Iraqi troops either surrendered or retreated, Operation Desert Storm ended, six weeks after the fighting began. Kuwait's independence had been restored and the Iraqi army, once the fourth largest in the world, was seemingly broken.

A NEW CENTURY BEGINS

In the aftermath of the war, the Iraqi people struggled to rebuild their cities and their lives. They suffered from poverty, malnutrition, and disease. Saddam Hussein and his supporters claimed that the UN sanctions were responsible for the suffering of his people, but the truth was not so simple. Saddam's focus was not on providing food and medicine for his people; he concentrated instead on spending vast sums of money to rebuild the Iraqi military and continuing to enrich himself and his closest supporters.

Ultimately, the UN passed a resolution lifting certain portions of the trade embargo (food and money, in particular) in exchange for Iraq meeting certain conditions, among them that Iraq take steps to destroy or remove all chemical, biological, and nuclear weapons under the supervision of UN inspectors. But initial attempts to inspect Saddam's weapons production facilities did not succeed. UN inspectors claimed that they were receiving incomplete lists of exactly where all such facilities were located, or they were being denied access when they arrived at the facilities. The United States, led by then-president Bill Clinton, wanted to punish Saddam for his clear violation of UN orders, but the coalition of countries that had stood up to Saddam when he overran Kuwait and threatened Saudi Arabia was less willing to back up UN demands this time. When Saddam ultimately ordered the UN inspectors to leave his country, claiming that they were merely U.S. spies, the Clinton administration could not rally a large group of nations to denounce Iraqi actions. Instead, as the international community witnessed the hardships the Iraqi people were suffering—hospitals without medicine, schools without supplies, families without food—it was less willing to embark on a bombing campaign that would, inevitably, visit even greater suffering upon the helpless citizens of this troubled nation.

The violence did not cease with the end of the Gulf War. Following Saddam's expulsion of the UN inspectors in October 1998, all UN staff members were evacuated from Baghdad. From December 16 to 19, 1998, U.S. and British forces launched a bombing campaign, known as Operation Desert Fox, designed to destroy Iraq's nuclear, chemical, and biological weapons' facilities. The missiles, while successfully targeting several sites, were nevertheless unable to effectively eliminate the capacity of the Iraqi government to develop these weapons of mass destruction.

10

The Costs of Conflict

On March 17, 2003, President George W. Bush delivered a televised address to the American people. The speech outlined his belief that diplomatic efforts to resolve conflicts with Iraq had not been successful, and that military action might be necessary to overthrow the regime of Saddam Hussein. President Bush's speech marked a fundamental shift in American foreign policy, not only toward Iraq, but toward any nation whose intent toward the United States might be hostile.

This change in foreign policy was a direct result of the terrorist attacks on the United States that took place on September 11, 2001. On that date, attacks by members of the terrorist network known as al Qaeda destroyed the two World Trade Center towers in New York and severely damaged the Pentagon in Washington, D.C., costing thouands of lives and dramatically challenging Americans' complacency about their security. Al Qaeda claimed no single country for its base, but instead it existed as a network of terrorist cells operating in multiple locations around the world.

In order to respond to the threat posed by al Qaeda and other terrorist groups, President Bush and his foreign policy advisers decided to adopt a more aggressive response to terrorism. Rather than relying on defensive and diplomatic postures, these political leaders determined to pursue the terrorist networks around the world and, at the same time, respond with force to those groups and countries that posed a potential threat to American security, rather than waiting for them to strike.

This position led the United States into war with Iraq in 2003. Intelligence reports suggested that Iraq, under Saddam Hussein, had continued to develop and possess what were labeled "weapons of mass destruction"—chemical and biological weapons—and was pursuing a policy to develop nuclear weapons. Intelligence reports also suggested—but never ultimately proved—a possible link between the Iraqi regime and members of the al Qaeda network, leading to the belief that Iraq might use these weapons against the United States or might sell them to terrorists who would use them against the United States.

As President Bush stated in his speech, "Instead of drifting along toward tragedy, we will set a course toward safety. Before the day of horror can come, before it is too late to act, this danger will be removed."

In his speech, Bush noted more specifically that part of the U.S. goal would be to remove Saddam Hussein from power. "Should Saddam Hussein choose confrontation, the American people should know that every measure has been taken to avoid war, and every measure will be taken to win it."

A TRAGEDY UNFOLDS

After the war in Iraq had begun, investigations by the Senate Select Committee on Intelligence and other groups revealed that this prewar intelligence was flawed. No evidence of existing weapons of mass destruction were found in Iraq when U.S. troops swept into the country.

The United States, seeking the support of other nations in its efforts to confront Saddam, had made arguments in the UN and sought through diplomatic means to force Iraq to cooperate more fully with UN weapons inspectors. The goal was to build the type of international coalition that the first president Bush had shaped during the conflict with Iraq over its invasion of Kuwait.

But these efforts were not as successful. Apart from the United Kingdom (UK), the United States was unable to attract significant partners this time; most of the countries that did agree to participate put severe restrictions on the numbers of troops they would commit and how and when those troops could be used.

The initial phase of the war lasted 21 days, from March 20 to April 9, 2003. The Iraqi army contained 400,000 soldiers, but the U.S.-led military effort began with an overwhelming initial bombardment, and rather than unleashing the expected chemical or biological weapons, or staging a dramatic defense of the capital, the Iraqi forces largely melted away, disappearing back into the population.

By April 9, Baghdad had been seized, and Saddam Hussein went into hiding. American military officials distributed packs of cards, each with the likeness of an Iraqi military leader or senior member of Saddam's regime. These were the "Most Wanted" in Iraq, with Saddam Hussein being number one, and his two sons, Uday and Qusay, numbers two and three, respectively.

For those living in Iraq, the war produced a dramatic change in daily life. In Baghdad, the war began before dawn on March 20 with the wail of air-raid sirens, red tracers flashing through the sky, and the sound of explosions throughout the city. Sites linked to the government and Saddam—especially his palaces—were the primary targets during the initial bombings. But civilians still were injured and killed, both by coalition attacks and by the Iraqi antiaircraft missiles. Many chose to flee the city.

Oil fires were set by Iraqi forces around Baghdad to interfere with American remote guidance systems. Thick smoke filled the streets, casting an eerie shadow over the city. Few of the Iraqis still remaining in Baghdad ventured out of their homes.

U.S. forces eventually bombed power stations, depriving the city of electricity and phone service. As American troops neared Baghdad, Iraqi forces staged a final series of futile efforts before disappearing. The capture of Baghdad was swift but bloody; hospitals were quickly overwhelmed by military casualties and wounded civilians caught in the crossfire.

By April 9, the Iraqi troops disappeared, along with police and senior members of the Ba'ath Party. In this absence of authority, looting quickly broke out. Groups broke into government buildings and warehouses, stealing computers, furniture, cars, and air

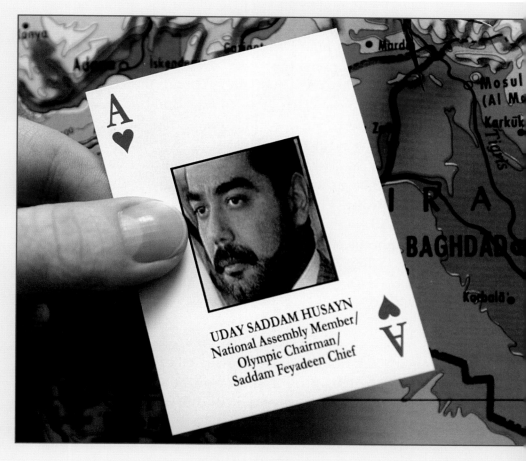

A crucial strategy in the 2003 U.S. attack on Iraq was to destroy everyone in Saddam Hussein's inner circle, not just the leader himself. Pictures of the ministers and officials who were heavily involved in Hussein's government were printed on a deck of cards, including Uday Hussein, Saddam Hussein's son.

conditioners. Some government offices were set on fire. Priceless and irreplaceable treasures were stolen from the Iraqi national museum, the national library, and government archives, evidence of Iraq's glorious past lost to looters and thieves.

The scenes of chaos were initially interpreted as joyous celebration, and U.S. soldiers did not interfere. But the impression conveyed to Iraqis, and to the world watching the riotous behavior on television, was of disorder—the invading forces were not in control of the country. Even those Iraqis who were glad that Saddam had been overthrown were troubled by the anarchy and violence, and by the sight of foreign troops moving through their streets. The only clearly guarded Iraqi building was the Oil Ministry, seeming to support the rumors that Americans had invaded Iraq to seize its oil.

On May 1, President Bush publicly announced that the combat phase of the war was over with the infamous phrase "Mission Accomplished." His words would prove sadly premature; the conflict in Iraq was only beginning. Three years after the president announced the war had ended, the dead and injured of the U.S. military numbered 20,000, with 95 percent of the casualties occurring after Baghdad had fallen.

A GUERRILLA WAR

The United States had attacked Iraq with a fairly specific plan for the defeat of the Iraqi army and the overthrow of Saddam, and these goals were accomplished quickly. But an apparent lack of adequate planning for what would follow that defeat resulted in a tragic series of events that continues to threaten Iraq's stability and the prospects for peace in the region.

There were several facets of the American occupation of Iraq that sparked a guerrilla war that has more recently widened into what can only be described as a civil war. First, was the lack of a decisive response to the looting and arson that followed the fall of Baghdad. Second, the United States had planned to form a new Iraqi government consisting of a group of Iraqi exiles who had been identified prior to the war and who would, it was believed, enact policies that would prove friendly to U.S. interests. But these leaders had, for the most part, lived much of their lives in countries other than Iraq. They had not suffered under Saddam and were resented by those who had. They lacked the ability to make quick decisions, and they focused on jostling for power rather than forming successful political coalitions that could govern.

Third, U.S. planning relied on the quick establishment of an Iraqi police and military presence, which would maintain law and order in the country and enable the swift drawing down of American troops. But the existing army had largely disappeared when American forces entered Baghdad. They and all members of the Ba'ath party were essentially fired by an official decree when L. Paul Bremer III, the American head of the Coalition Provisional Authority brought in to restore order to the chaotic situation in Baghdad, took office on May 12. Bremer's decision to dissolve the Iraqi army and remove former members of the Ba'ath Party from its upper ranks created mass unemployment throughout Iraq. Many people had been forced to join the party in order to obtain any kind of meaningful employment, and Bremer's decree not only laid off most of the trained Iraqi officers and policemen, but also doctors, teachers, engineers, and other professionals. According to one set of figures from the Ministry of Labor, approximately 70 percent of the work force (12 million people out of a population of 25 million) were unemployed in 2003.

Resentment at the American occupation quickly escalated. Food was in short supply; people were out of work and unpaid. Electricity was sporadic; hospitals lacked needed power to operate equipment. Iraqis sweltered in un-air conditioned homes and buildings while temperatures soared well above 100°F.

In addition, the quality of life for the average Iraqi was noticeably worse under the American occupation than it had been while Saddam was in power. Before the overthrow of Saddam, 50 percent of Iraqis had access to drinkable water; this figure dropped to 32 percent by the end of 2005. Electricity was well below preinvasion levels, approximately half of what was needed in the country. Attacks on oil fields by guerrilla forces resulted in a drop in oil production. Iraq was a dangerous place, made more dangerous by the advent of suicide bombers and buried bombs known as improvised explosive devices

(IEDs), which were generally an explosive device detonated by remote control.

Initially, it was the 5 million Sunni Arabs who were alienated. The majority Shiites were angered by the occupation but initially hoped to benefit in the long term from national elections promised by the Americans. However, as the violence and despair spread throughout Iraq, bands of Sunnis and Shiites were soon fighting the Americans, and each other.

The economic collapse of Iraq had begun well before the American invasion. Decades of war had decimated much of the economy. UN sanctions had broken what remained. The middle class of Iraq had largely disappeared, and Iraq was divided between the small minority who had benefited from Saddam's reign and the vast majority who had not. Under Saddam's three decades of rule, Iraq had existed as a society strongly governed by the desires and dictates of one man. When this authority was removed, chaos immediately resulted.

CAPTURING TYRANTS

The U.S. military offered a reward of $15 million each for information leading to the capture of Saddam Hussein's two sons, Uday (age 39) and Qusay (age 37), who were even more ruthless and brutal than their father had been. For many Iraqis, Uday and Qusay exemplified the most violent aspects of their father's reign.

Qusay was believed to be Saddam's intended successor. He headed Iraq's intelligence and security services, including the Republican Guard and its units responsible for protecting the Iraqi leadership. UN weapons inspectors also believed that Qusay was responsible for overseeing the development of any unconventional weapons in Iraq. Qusay was given control of the army by his father in 2000, and before the invasion was charged with protecting Baghdad.

Uday, the oldest of Saddam's children, had survived an assassination attempt in 1996 that left him partially handicapped. He kidnapped and tortured countless Iraqis and, as head of Iraq's National Olympic Committee, jailed and tortured athletes who had lost important games.

On July 23, 2003, the U.S. military received a tip from an Iraqi informant that Uday and Qusay were hiding in a home in Mosul

After coalition forces captured them, Saddam Hussein *(seated, bottom right)* and his eight co-defendants were placed on trial in Iraq. Knowing the Iraqi people were intently watching the trial, Hussein pled innocent to charges of mass killings and attacks against certain groups in his country and used the live broadcast to deliver speeches. He was later convicted for his crimes and executed.

in northern Iraq. U.S. troops surrounded the home and called on the men to surrender, but instead there was an exchange of gunfire, and the two sons of Saddam were killed. Iraqis initially refused to believe that the two men had been killed until newspapers and television stations published graphic photos showing their bullet-riddled bodies.

Five months later, U.S. forces successfully located and captured Saddam Hussein, marking a distinct end to his hold on power.

Saddam Hussein ultimately was tried in Iraqi courts for crimes committed during his reign. His first trial began in October 2005, and it concerned Saddam's role in the execution of 148 men and boys in the mostly Shiite village of Dujail in 1982 for having tried to assassinate him. The trial lasted nine months and was marked by numerous security breaches. Three defense lawyers were assassinated during the course of the trial; the first chief judge resigned, noting that he was tired of criticism from Iraqi officials of his handling of the case. Saddam and his eight codefendants frequently disrupted the court with outbursts challenging the legitimacy of the trial. Although the chief judge's identity was released, the names of his four co-judges were kept private to protect them against the threat of assassination.

Saddam's defense was that he did not know about the killings, but the prosecution produced his signature on orders of execution. He clashed with the chief judge from the beginning; when he was identified as the "former president," he responded fiercely that he was still "the president" of Iraq. The trial ended with a sentence of death by hanging for Saddam Hussein.

The execution order was ultimately signed by the recently elected Iraqi prime minister Nuri al-Maliki. Shortly before dawn on December 30, 2006, after 1,000 days in solitary confinement in an American-run detention center, Saddam was taken from his cell and driven to northern Baghdad, where he was officially handed over to Iraqi custody.

Witnesses and the evidence from the cell phone of one of those present have shown that Saddam was taunted as he prayed.

Saddam initially replied that he had nothing to apologize for when asked if he felt any remorse. A black cloth was wound around his neck, and the taunts from several of those present continued during Saddam's final moments. At one point, Saddam was heard muttering "Gallows of shame," before praying. After his execution, one witness was heard calling out, "The tyrant has fallen."

IRAQ AFTER SADDAM HUSSEIN

If U.S. hopes had been pinned on a reduction of violence after Saddam's execution, they were disappointed. The news of his execution marked a sharpening divide between those Shiite Iraqis who had been oppressed under his regime, and those Sunnis who feared their reprisals. The Kurds, who had been victims in several of Saddam's most violent attacks, were disappointed that he was hanged before he stood trial for the mass killings and chemical attacks on Kurdish villages.

But the question of how Iraq would be governed, and what would bring the violence to an end, continued to challenge Iraqis and Americans alike. The violence endangered everyone, leaving few untouched. In August 2003, a truck bomb destroyed part of the UN headquarters in Baghdad, killing Brazilian Sergio Vieira de Mello, UN Special Representative to Iraq, and 16 others. This attack prompted the UN and other aid agencies to begin pulling their representatives out of Iraq.

In late April 2004, photos became public showing that Iraqi prisoners in Abu Ghraib prison had been subjected to humiliation and torture at the hands of American military personnel. The photos sparked public debate about the use of torture by the United States and caused many around the world to question what had happened to the American goals of an invasion designed to spread freedom and democracy.

On June 28, 2004, L. Paul Bremer officially handed over sovereignty in Iraq to a transitional government, with Iyad Allawi as interim prime minister. The plan was for this government to hold power until a new one was chosen after an election in January 2005. Many were suspicious of Allawi's obvious ties to Washington. The handing over of sovereignty did not mean an end to the U.S. military presence in Iraq. Allawi's government faced constant threats, including the efforts of radical cleric Muqtada al-Sadr and his Shiite militia. U.S. troops engaged in a fierce fight with al-Sadr's militia in the city of Najaf in August 2004, a fight that ended only when Iraq's most senior cleric, Grand Ayatollah Ali al-Sistani, intervened and brokered a cease-fire. One of the terms was that Sadr, who had been wanted by the U.S. military on murder charges, would instead be allowed to participate in Iraq's political process.

On January 30, 2005, Iraq held its first democratic elections in 50 years. Despite a Sunni boycott of the elections and sporadic violence, a respectable number of Iraqis chose to cast a ballot. The United Iraqi Alliance, a coalition of Shiite politicians, won the largest number of votes in the National Assembly election, leading to the nomination of Jalal Talabani, a Kurd, to be Iraq's president. Still, the votes reflected the religious and ethnic background of most voters, deepening the divide in Iraqi politics.

Bombings in the ensuing months targeted anyone believed to be cooperating with the American authorities, as well as holy Shiite and Sunni sites. The golden-domed al-Askari mosque in Samarra, one of the holiest Shiite shrines, was damaged in a bombing. Reprisal attacks on Sunni mosques quickly followed. In only a few days in February 2006, more than 1,300 Iraqis died.

Parliamentary elections in December 2005 led to intense debate over who would be the next prime minister of Iraq. Shiite Ibrahim al-Jaafari had served before, but his time in office marked a period of widening divisions between the various factions within Iraq, Jaafari failed to deliver on promises he had made to the Kurds who formed part of his political coalition, and Jaafari's connections to Muqtada al-Sadr were troubling to those who feared the radical cleric's influence on Iraqi politics.

Despite the conflict and unrest throughout the country, Iraqis braved security threats in order to vote at their local polling center. Many citizens remain dedicated to the idea of an independent, democratic government and actively take part in the election process. Here, a man in Basra dips his finger in purple ink, signifying that he has already cast his ballot.

Finally, Nuri al-Maliki was chosen as the new prime minister. Shortly after forming his new government, al-Maliki delivered a bold promise: Iraq's forces would be strong enough to keep peace in the country by the end of 2007, enabling the withdrawal of U.S. forces.

In January 2007, troubled by the increasing violence and growing anti-American sentiment throughout the Middle East, as well as rising pressure within the United States to bring American troops home, President Bush decided to increase the number of U.S. troops in Iraq. He hoped that the greater numbers would be able to keep the country from collapsing in civil war. As part of a shift in political and military strategy, President Bush committed an additional 21,500 U.S. troops in Iraq in what he labeled "The New Way Forward." Part of the mission was to bring down the levels of violence in order to enable Prime Minister al-Maliki to take steps toward reconciliation of all of the different factions in Iraq. Much of the focus was on stabilizing Baghdad—30,000 American troops were stationed in Baghdad alone.

The troop surge succeeded partially in areas where greater numbers were stationed, but the lawlessness and violence spread to the more remote areas where fewer American troops were stationed. With the Iraqi government seemingly unable to stop the chaos, many began to question when American troops should leave Iraq and what would happen when they did.

A DISTANT PEACE

Iraq faces an uncertain future. Violence between Shiites and Sunnis has ripped apart once peaceful neighborhoods, devolving into civil war as a weak government struggles to maintain control. American troops patrol the streets and are themselves the target of much of the violence. The American presence in Iraq cost $10 billion a month in late 2007, with those expenses likely to increase. Thousands of Iraqis and Americans had lost their lives since the war began, and much of Iraq's infrastructure had been destroyed by the war and its aftermath.

The crisis facing Iraq has certain basic elements. The government has been weakened by sectarian divisions, with the leadership failing to act in ways that advance Iraq's best interests. The government has not managed to achieve any kind of national reconciliation, to ensure basic security, or to provide the Iraqi people with basic services.

Neighboring countries, such as Syria and Iran, have not helped Iraq achieve stability but, instead, may be aiding insurgent elements in ways that are adding to the crisis. The Iraqi military lacks leadership, equipment, personnel, and support. The Iraqi police are unable to control crime.

The greatest violence in Iraq has come from within. Sunni Arab insurgents and Shiite militias and death squads repeatedly clash. The terrorist group al Qaeda and other jihadist groups have exploited Iraq's chaos and now are believed to be actively working in Iraq to encourage attacks against the U.S. troops based there.

Daily life remains harsh and dangerous for most ordinary Iraqis. Electricity is at best meeting about half the Iraqi people's needs, and it has fallen below the levels available before the U.S. invasion. Most of the country lacks effective sanitation. In September 2007, the Iraqi Ministry of Water Resources reported that only 32 percent of the population had access to clean drinking water and only 19 percent had access to good sewage systems. In that same period, Iraqi numbers reported more than 60,000 civilian deaths since the war began, with some estimates much higher.

Iraq has the third largest proven crude oil reserves in the world, but years of sanctions and underinvestment have crippled the industry. Attacks on oil and gas pipelines and personnel have cost Iraq billions of dollars in lost revenue, and oil exports in 2007 were well below what they had been before the American invasion.

UN figures in 2007 showed that one-quarter of the Iraqi population depended on food rations. Education is another area of concern. Literacy rates are dropping; many of Iraq's schools have needed to be rehabilitated or rebuilt. Many schools have closed because of bombings, kidnappings, and threats to teachers and students. Figures from the United Nations Children's Fund (UNICEF) show that 75 percent of children are not attending school in Baghdad.

The twenty-first century is now well under way, but Iraq's current condition has crippled its efforts to play a leading role in the modern Middle East. This legacy, shaped by the hastily drawn borders that defined the nation in the aftermath of World War I, are now played out in the sectarian violence threatening stability. Many of the problems created after World War I, when British politicians first tried to define exactly where the nation to be known as Iraq would begin and end, spark violence among Iraqis today.

Perhaps most tragically, Iraq has witnessed many of the same mistakes being repeated in its most recent history. Well-intentioned Western powers, attempting to build a lasting government in Iraq, one that would be friendly to their interests, have failed to create stability or lasting support for their efforts. Each time Iraq has attempted to transition to independence from these powers, the result has been systems of government unable to handle the strain of competing political goals. The period in which Saddam Hussein led the country was marked by violence, terror, and oppression for much of the Iraqi population, but with his removal from power a vacuum has been created, which numerous competing interests have attempted to fill. The civil war that has resulted now threatens not only Iraq's future, but the future of much of the Middle East as well.

Chronology

1920	Iraq is mandated to Britain.
1921	Faisal becomes the first king of Iraq on August 23.
1925	A constitution is adopted, specifying that Iraq will be a monarchy.
1932	Iraq is admitted to the League of Nations.
1933	Iraqi troops brutally massacre Assyrians living in the north. King Faisal resigns and dies; his son Ghazi becomes king.
1937	Saddam Hussein is born in Tikrit.
1939	King Ghazi dies in a car accident; four-year-old Faisal II becomes king.
1941	British troops arrive at military base at Habbaniya; Iraqi military attempts to block additional forces. Britain attacks and establishes new government in Baghdad.
1942	Iraq declares war on Germany and officially enters World War II.
1945	Political parties are formed to strengthen the parliamentary system.
1953	King Faisal II turns 18 and officially assumes rule over Iraq.
1958	Militia marches on Baghdad and seizes power. Royal family is killed. Iraq is declared a republic, and Qasim becomes head of government.
1963	Ba'ath Party overthrows government. Qasim is executed. Nine months later, Arif and military officers overthrow Ba'athist government.
1966	Arif is killed in a helicopter crash. His older brother becomes president.
1968	Ba'ath Party seizes power. General al-Bakr becomes president.
1972	Iraq nationalizes the Iraq Petroleum Company.

1979   Saddam Hussein becomes president.

1980   Iran–Iraq War begins.

1988   Cease-fire goes into effect. Saddam launches chemical weapons attack against Kurdish villages.

1990   Iraq invades Kuwait. UN condemns the action and later calls for economic sanctions against Iraq.

1991   UN forces launch attack against Iraq (Operation Desert Storm). War lasts for six weeks before ending when Kuwaiti independence is restored.

1996   UN and Iraq agree that Iraq will be allowed to export oil to buy food and medicine.

1998   Iraq refuses to cooperate with UN weapons inspectors. U.S. and British forces launch bombing campaign

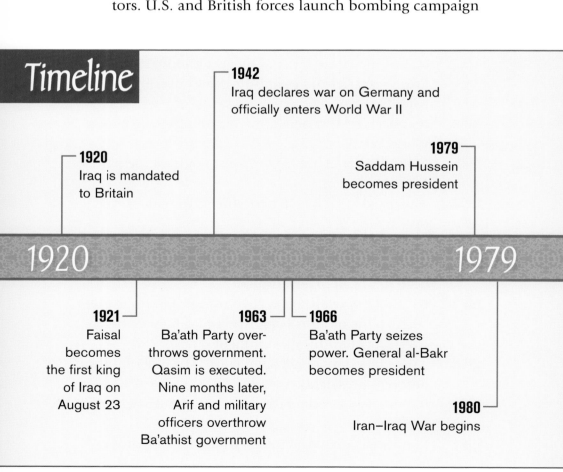

Timeline

1942
Iraq declares war on Germany and officially enters World War II

1920
Iraq is mandated to Britain

1979
Saddam Hussein becomes president

1920   1979

1921
Faisal becomes the first king of Iraq on August 23

1963
Ba'ath Party overthrows government. Qasim is executed. Nine months later, Arif and military officers overthrow Ba'athist government

1966
Ba'ath Party seizes power. General al-Bakr becomes president

1980
Iran–Iraq War begins

(Operation Desert Fox) to destroy Iraq's nuclear, chemical, and biological weapons facilities.

2000   Baghdad airport reopens, and Iraq resumes domestic passenger flights.

2001   U.S. and British forces launch bombing attacks near Baghdad.

2003   U.S. and coalition forces attack Iraq on March 20. Saddam's government is toppled on April 9. Saddam's sons are killed on July 22. Saddam is captured on December 13.

2004   Photographs showing American military personnel abuse of Iraqi prisoners at Abu Ghraib are made public in April. In May, Iyad Allawi is named interim prime

1990
Iraq invades Kuwait. UN condemns the action and later calls for economic sanctions against Iraq

1991
UN forces launch attack against Iraq (Operation Desert Storm). War lasts for six weeks before ending when Kuwaiti independence is restored

2003
U.S. and coalition forces attack Iraq on March 20. Saddam's government is toppled on April 9

1990

2006

1998
Iraq refuses to cooperate with UN weapons inspectors. U.S. and British forces launch bombing campaign (Operation Desert Fox) to destroy Iraq's nuclear, chemical, and biological weapons facilities

2006
Nuri al-Maliki is chosen prime minister in April after months of deadlock. Saddam is executed on December 31

minister. On June 28, United States hands power over to interim government.

2005   In January, Iraqis vote in first democratic election in 50 years. In October, trial of Saddam Hussein begins.

2006   Samarra shrine is bombed in February. Nuri al-Maliki is chosen prime minister in April after months of deadlock. Saddam is executed on December 30.

2007   President Bush announces substantial increase in U.S. troops in Iraq in January. Prime Minister al-Maliki declares that Iraq will be responsible for its own security by end of year.

Bibliography

Associated Press. "Smithsonian Displays Relics of Iraqi Queen from 4,500 Years Ago," October 15, 1999. Available online. URL: http://www.geocities.com/Iraqinfo/index. html?page=/Iraqinfo/sum/southern-iraq/ur.html.

Bell, Florence, ed. *The Letters of Gertrude Bell*. Vol. 1. New York: Boni and Liveright, 1927.

Bremer, L. Paul III, with Malcolm McConnell. *My Year in Iraq*. New York: Simon & Schuster, 2006.

Bulloch, John, and Harvey Morris. *Saddam's War*. Boston: Faber & Faber, 1991.

Burns, John F. "First Court Case of Hussein Stems from Killings in Village in '82," *The New York Times*, June 6, 2005. Available online. URL: http://www.nytimes.com/2005/06/06/international/middleeast/06trial.html.

———. "Hussein Video Grips Iraq; Attacks Go On," *The New York Times*, December 31, 2006. Available online. URL: http://www.nytimes.com/2006/12/31/world/middleeast/31iraq.html?_r=1&pagewanted=2&oref=slogin.

———. "Transition in Iraq: The Departing Administrator," *The New York Times*, June 29, 2004. Available online. URL: http://query.nytimes.com/gst/fullpage.html?res=9A02E6DF1538F93AA15755C0A9629C8B63.

Cave, Damien, and Stephen Farrell. "At Street Level, Unmet Goals of Troop Buildup," *The New York Times*, September 9, 2007. Available online. URL: http://www.nytimes.com/2007/09/09/world/middleeast/09surge.html.

Christie, Agatha. *An Autobiography*. New York: Dodd, Mead & Co., 1977.

Cockburn, Patrick. *The Occupation: War and Resistance in Iraq*. New York: Verso, 2006.

Dudley, William, ed. *Iraq: Opposing Viewpoints*. San Diego, Calif.: Greenhaven Press, 2004.

Fromkin, David. *A Peace to End All Peace*. New York: Avon Books, 1989.

Garrels, Anne. *Naked in Baghdad: The Iraq War as Seen by NPR's Correspondent*. New York: Farrar, Straus & Giroux, 2003.

Gibbs, Nancy. "Saddam's Capture," *Time*, December 22, 2003. Available online. URL: http://www.time.com/time/magazine/article/0,9171,1066488,00.html.

Hermann, Peter. "Arab Newspapers Minimize Arrest, Focus on Occupation," *Baltimore Sun*, December 16, 2003. Available online. URL: http://www.baltimoresun.com/news/nationworld/iraq/balte.press16dec16,0,3158713.story.

Iraq Study Group. *The Iraq Study Group Report: The Way Forward—A New Approach*. New York: Vintage Books, 2006.

Karsh, Efraim, and Inari Rautsi. *Saddam Hussein*. New York: Free Press, 1991.

Keegan, John. *The Iraq War*. New York: Alfred A. Knopf, 2004.

Khadduri, Majid. *The Gulf War*. New York: Oxford University Press, 1988.

———. *Republican Iraq*. New York: Oxford University Press, 1969.

———. *Socialist Iraq*. Washington, D.C.: The Middle East Institute, 1978.

Khalidi, Walid. "Iraq vs. Kuwait: Claims and Counterclaims." In *The Gulf War Reader*. Sifry, M.L., and C. Cerf, eds. New York: Times Books, 1991.

Kramer, Samuel Noah. *The Sumerians*. Chicago: University of Chicago Press, 1963.

MacFarquhar, Neil. "After the War: Iraq; Hussein's 2 Sons Dead in Shootout, U.S. Says," *The New York Times*, July 23, 2003. Available online. URL: http://query.nytimes.com/gst/fullpage.html?res=9C05E7DA143FF930A15754C0A9659C8B63.

———. "Saddam Hussein, Defiant Dictator Who Ruled Iraq with Violence and Fear, Dies," *The New York Times*, December 30, 2006. Available online. URL: http://www.nytimes.com/2006/12/30/world/middleeast/30saddam.html.

Miller, Judith, and Laurie Mylroie. "The Rise of Saddam Hussein." In *The Gulf War Reader*. Sifry, M.L., and C. Cerf, eds. New York: Times Books, 1991.

Morgan, Janet. *Agatha Christie: A Biography*. New York: Alfred A. Knopf, 1985.

Packer, George. *The Assassins' Gate: America in Iraq*. New York: Farrar, Straus & Giroux, 2005.

Preston, Julia. "Hussein Trial Was Flawed but Reasonably Fair, and Verdict Was Justified, Legal Experts Say," *The New York Times*, November 6, 2006. Available online. URL: http://www.nytimes.com/2006/11/06/world/middleeast/06trial.html.

Sachs, Susan. "The Capture of Hussein: Ex-Dictator; Hussein Caught in Makeshift Hide-out; Bush Says 'Dark Era' for Iraqis Is Over," *The New York Times*, December 15, 2003. Available online. URL: http://query.nytimes.com/gst/fullpage.html?res=9C07EEDA103CF936A25751C1A9659C8B63.

Select Committee on Intelligence of the U.S. Senate. *Report on the U.S. Intelligence Community's Prewar Intelligence Assessments on Iraq*. 108th Congress, 2nd Session, S. Report 108-301, July 9, 2004.

Silverfarb, Daniel. *The Twilight of British Ascendancy in the Middle East*. New York: St. Martin's Press, 1994.

Simon, Reeva S. *Iraq Between the Two World Wars*. New York: Columbia University Press, 1986.

Tavernise, Sabrina. "Hussein Divides Iraq, Even in Death," *The New York Times*, December 31, 2006. Available online. URL: http://www.nytimes.com/2006/12/31/world/middleeast/31voices.html.

Von Zielbauer, Paul. "For Hussein, a Long, Raucous Trial Ends in His Absence," *The New York Times*, July 28, 2006. Available online. URL: http://www.nytimes.com/2006/07/28/world/middleeast/28iraq.html?n=Top/Reference/Times%20Topics/People/Z/Zielbauer,%20Paul%20von.

Waas, Murray. "What Washington Gave Saddam for Christmas." In *The Gulf War Reader*. Sifry, M.L., and C. Cerf, eds. New York: Times Books, 1991.

Wallach, Janet. *Desert Queen*. New York: Anchor Books, 1996.

Wellard, James. *Babylon*. New York: Saturday Review Press, 1972.

Young, Gavin. *Iraq: Land of Two Rivers*. London: Collins St. James Place, 1980.

Web Sites:

www.arab.net

www.baghdad.com

www.britannica.com

www.news.bbc.co.uk

www.npr.org

www.nytimes.com

www.time.com

Further Resources

Butler, Richard. *The Greatest Threat*. New York: Public Affairs, 2000.

Dudley, William, ed. *Iraq: Opposing Viewpoints*. San Diego, Calif.: Greenhaven Press, 2004.

Schomp, Virginia. *Ancient Mesopotamia*. New York: Scholastic, 2004.

Simon, Reeva S. *Iraq Between the Two World Wars*. New York: Columbia University Press, 1986.

Taus-Bolstad, Stacy. *Iraq in Pictures*. Minneapolis, Minn.: Lerner Publications, 2004.

Web Sites:

BBC Country Profile: Iraq
http://www.news.bbc.co.uk/2/hi/country_profiles/791014.stm

CNN: Iraq—Transition of Power
http://www.cnn.com/SPECIALS/2005/iraq.transition/

National Public Radio: The Iraq War
http://www.npr.org/templates/topics/topic.php?topicId=1010

The New York Times: Times Topics: Iraq
http://topics.nytimes.com/top/news/international/countriesandterritories/iraq/index.html?scp=1-spot&sq=iraq&st=cse

U.S. Department of State: Iraq
http://www.state.gov/p/nea/ci/c3212.htm

The World News Network: Iraq Agency
http://www.iraqagency.com

Picture Credits

Index

About the Contributors

Author **Heather Lehr Wagner** is an editor and writer. She has an M.A. in government from the College of William and Mary and a B.A. in political science from Duke University. She is the author of more than 40 books exploring political and social issues, including several other volumes in the CREATION OF THE MODERN MIDDLE EAST series.

Series editor **Arthur Goldschmidt Jr.** is a retired professor of Middle East History at Penn State University. He has a B.A. in economics from Colby College and his M.A. and Ph.D. degrees from Harvard University in history and Middle Eastern Studies. He is the author of *A Concise History of the Middle East*, which has gone through eight editions, and many books, chapters, and articles about Egypt and other Middle Eastern countries. His most recent publication is *A Brief History of Egypt*, published by Facts On File in 2008. He lives in State College, Pennsylvania, with his wife, Louise. They have two grown sons.